THE CALM PLACE

DISCOVERING NATURE IN A YEAR LIKE NO OTHER

JACKIE KIRKHAM

CONTENTS

Introduction

I t started as the simplest of ideas. I wanted to write and improve how I describe the seemingly simple, elevating it to something special. I didn't need to go on a fancy quest or far away, just somewhere nearby and pleasant enough that I knew changed over the year, so I could get better at noticing stuff and writing about it. In my reading life, I'd also found myself drawn to accounts of nature and place and thought one day I might like to add to that canon. So I hatched a plan: a year in my garden, watching it change and grow, and recording it in my notebook. I couldn't afford a Creative Writing MFA, but this could be the next best thing.

New Year's Day, 2020. My Facebook status? "Happy New Year! May 2020 be infinitely better than 2019 for us all." When I started this project, I had no idea it would come to mean so much more in the midst of the chaos of, well, 2020.

We're lucky to have a garden, but it's not what you'd describe as extensive. Out the back, we have a courtyard shared with four other houses, covered in tarmac and home to a set of washing lines, plus a few pots with plants in varying stages of neglect and a raised bed where we grow a few vegetables every year. Even with my capacity for nerdily noticing minutiae, I would find that hard-going for an entire year. Out the front, a not-quite-enclosed garden which is all ours, about five by six metres total. It's got a few mature bushes, a tough-as-old-boots clematis, some rampaging ivy, some bird feeders and a scruffy lawn which, however hard I try, can't help but lower the tone of the neighbourhood. A bit more promising, but whatever I came up with, it was unlikely to be a literary masterpiece with this material. But that was okay—this was for my eyes only, a record of the garden and a record of my hopefully improving eye for detail and description. Nobody else would ever read it.

I'm not an avid or particularly skilled gardener, but when I lived in London I moved to a property whose garden consisted of a concrete patio and a biggish patch of mud which the Housing Association hadn't quite got round to turfing. Something clicked. The next four years saw me digging, planting, scrounging cuttings, sowing seeds, laying a gravel path, and making compost, and I was hooked. It was never going to win awards anywhere, it was far too chaotic for that. Still, it was my space to learn and grow and breathe, a space to leave behind the stresses of London living, at least for a while. As well as missing my friends when I left London to move to Scotland, leaving that garden was the biggest wrench, and I still feel wistful when I think about it and wonder what it's like now.

For my first few years after moving from London I didn't have a garden, not really. My Glasgow tenement flat had a shared back court and I put a few pot plants out there (most of them died), but other than occasionally hanging out my washing, or taking the rubbish out to the bins, I had to make do with the local park (which luckily was magnificent) for my outdoor fix. It was lovely, but not the same.

In time, I made use of a guerrilla garden a few minutes' walk away: a tiny patch of wasteland between a couple of tenements, which a local Glasgow community group had reclaimed and was using for planting, composting, and providing work experience for clients who were down on their luck. It was an oasis in an area of deprivation, a lovely patch of colour in a vibrant but slightly tatty neighbourhood, and I loved that I could take my old vegetable peelings to their compost heap and give them back to nature. Of course, developers found it eventually, and the group were evicted so a residential home could be built for people with dementia. Something that's much needed, definitely, but there? Near a main road, no green space at all to sit in, just somewhere to shut them away. I was sad for the garden, and for the new residents. But I'll always be grateful for those couple of years, which showed so powerfully the difference a tiny bit of green space could make to a neighbourhood, and to the people in it.

A few years later, we moved out of the big city to a much smaller one, Stirling. Ideally, I'd have wanted a bigger garden, but it was the one tiny downside to a host of advantages, and I reasoned a tiny garden was better than nothing. A small front garden probably wouldn't be the green haven I craved, but it would do for the time being. I hoped it would at least be enough to ease the sense of disconnection between me and the natural world that urban and suburban life seems so good at fostering. So often in our urban areas, building up and out and on top of are prioritised over recognising the abundant life that gives so much pleasure and enriches both us and our natural environment. I'm as inspired as the next person by the plucky plant that forces its way through cracks in the tarmac, and am as liable as the next person to turn it into some trite, inspirational truism. But honestly: there's something about getting your hands dirty and watching something you tended growing and producing food, or a big old stop-what-you're-doing-and-look-at-me flower, or a gnarly bark face in an old tree, that just makes my soul soar. I hoped my little garden would be enough.

When I started my project of writing and noticing, the news of a new virus in China was worrying, but not obviously immediately relevant to my life on the other side of the world. I couldn't not think about it for long though. As the coronavirus spread westwards, we gradually all started waiting for the time when it would arrive in the UK, likely England first and then here in Scotland. Then the rumours started—there would be a lockdown, schools would close, people wouldn't be able to go to work, and for people like me who worked in the National Health Service, the threat/promise of redeployment to the front line. The collective anxiety was palpable, just below the surface. It was just a matter of time. What impact would this virus have on me, my family, our jobs, our communities? I tried not to think too much about it, to go with the flow, and hope the flow wouldn't engulf me.

The first couple of months in the garden that year, then, were a mixture of denial about what was going on in the world, and delight at the emerging signs of spring—earlier than I'd noticed them before. Was that because I was taking the time to notice, or was it really earlier because climate change was impacting even this far north? Either way, as those first budding leaves, increased birdsong and activity, and even the first bees started to reveal themselves, I relaxed, breathed, started to learn the patterns and rhythms of the garden, and allowed myself to feel rest and hope.

Come March, denial wasn't an option any more. As the global pandemic was declared, and the virus named COVID-19, society locked down. Like parents up and down the country, we prepared for home learning with apprehension.

My husband, HD, geared up for full-time working from home, and I got the email telling me that, twenty years after last working as a ward nurse, I was to put my research job on hold and return to the ward. It wasn't a designated covid ward, but none of us knew if or when we'd be taking covid patients, and what that would mean for us all. We all seemed to go into self-protection mode: heightened anxiety and hypervigilance, feeling our way as policies were revised daily with increased knowledge. At work and in society, we felt like we were under siege.

Added to all this, the reality of trying to home educate six-year-old DreamGirl, and explain what was happening in an age appropriate way when we barely knew ourselves, compounded the anxiety and brought the stress ever more into the foreground. I worried about her education, my inadequacy as a home educator, on top of the stress of work and societal change, fear of contagion, concern for far away family, and a general feeling of powerlessness and lack of control. Like pretty much everyone else, I needed to find somewhere, or some way, to escape, reset, and fill the mental well to enable me to get through this.

The garden—this tiny, insignificant, suburban few square metres—could not have been more different from the news, and it soon became a refuge. Pulsating with energy and purpose and new life, it constantly astounded me with its abundance and simplicity, and its contrast to our other daily reality. It helped clear my head, got me breathing more slowly, noticing not only what I could see but also how I felt. The daily doomscrolling obsession with death and sickness and societal stress came face to face with this tiny patch of thrumming, pulsating, in-your-face life. The fear and guilt and stress and reluctance of home learning was relieved in this place, where we could both learn and relax and get to know the lives with which we shared this space. After the stress and conflict of trying (and often failing) to persuade DreamGirl to just do one more activity, this was the place where we could reconnect, not just with nature but also with each other.

When I started this project, I hoped I would notice little things going on in the garden, and find ways to write about it, enjoying practising the craft of writing. I also hoped that I'd enjoy some moments of peace and quiet, and that the fresh air and sunlight (yes, even in Scotland) would help me feel better, both mentally and physically. I experienced all that and so, so much more.

As the world teetered in the confusion and uncertainty and fear of covid, unstable politicians, climate emergency, ongoing discrimination and conflict, this little postage stamp of ground became an anchor and a haven, as I got to know the characters of the birds and plants and other life that inhabited it. I gained a sense of rootedness in place, home, history, even as the world seemed to shrink.

It also—unexpectedly—unsettled me. It asked me difficult questions about community, about belonging, about privilege, and about my own personal ethics: not, it turned out, always as perfect and 'woke' as I'd like to think.

Ultimately, experiencing this same tiny plot of ground over the course of a year like no other taught me the importance of living in the now, of cultivating wonder and gratitude, of treasuring simplicity, of re-evaluating what significance and a life well-lived actually look like. But it also taught me the importance of appreciating how precarious and connected the world is, and how easy it is to exclude and limit true belonging.

At the end of the year, the last thing I wrote in my garden diary was this simple phrase:

I have enough.

It is my hope that this book captures some of that tension and wonder, and shows the amazing complexity of even the tiniest patches of our incredible natural world. I also hope that my voice can play a part in helping everyone, whatever their background or circumstances, discover the beauty all around them, on their doorsteps.

January

Something deeper lies behind the practicalities of learning to notice. As I get older, and see my young daughter growing up into her own person, I feel a strange urge to memorialise this life, at this time, and acknowledge its significance. Not that I have ideas above my station: I know in the cosmic scheme of things my little patch of existence is neither here nor there. But I have practical and emotional significance to my loved ones, including the responsibility to nurture my daughter and encourage her to be all she can be. On top of that, my creativity, the urge to share with others the beauty and bonkersness and awesomeness of this little bit of life, won't shut up and leave me alone. So here I am, recording the garden year, and hopefully learning and growing as a writer in the process.

Here in the northern reaches, the turn of the year can sometimes be crisp and clear and invigorating and inspirational. More often than not, the constant gloom leads many, including me, along the path of anxiety and fear. Fear that this will be the year that the warmth won't return, that nothing will ever change, that despite my pretensions I won't ever amount to much. This feels like one of those years, not helped by a creeping and incessant anxiety about impending environmental and political catastrophe. Maybe writing about my garden is the ultimate indulgence. Fiddling while Rome burns, gazing at my navel while the world goes to hell. Could I—should I—be doing something properly useful, instead of stroking my chin thinking how interesting I am? Sitting in the garden in the midst of this tension between wanting to express and improve my creativity and wondering what the point is of even bothering, I'm not sure I know where to start.

There's only so much you can fit in a five or six square metre front garden. A scrappy lawn that can comfortably fit three people on camping chairs, although four would be a squeeze. Some mature shrubs and bushes: a big cotoneaster under the front window, some unidentified bushes which, from left to right I refer to throughout this book as the toilet brush hedge, the sparrow hedge, the waxy leaved bush and the smelly bush[1] which separate us from the neighbours, and along the ivy-covered front wall a conifer, a ceanothus, and a giant hebe nine or ten feet both tall and wide. Added to that is a big clematis to the left of the front door, some straggly honeysuckle to the right, plus Next Door's tree. As I can see my neighbour's tree wherever I

---

1. . I've since learned that the smelly bush is a choisya (aka Mexican Orange), but the others remain unidentified.

sit, and it's enjoyed by the same birds that hang out in our garden, I consider it an honorary part of our garden too. A few seconds, and you've literally seen everything there is to see.

Wondering what to look at this first time out in the garden this year. What to notice, where to start? It's nearly 3:30 and it's getting dull already—skies are overcast, albeit with a tinge of pink over to the west which makes me think of Australia, burning even as I write with horrific bush fires over so much of the country. I must remember not only to not moan about Scotland's weather so much, but to give thanks that, for the most part, it doesn't try to burn us to oblivion.

It's so easy to think we're not linked to the rest of the world. We're our own little enclave and the only thing that matters is what happens here. This reminder of Australia, where friends face real danger while I sit by my front door indulging myself in a fantasy of becoming a fabulous writer, surprises me with its force. If that's what a tinge of pink sunlight on a cloud can do, what else is waiting for me here?

Crows cawing overhead, and cheeping from Next Door's garden—some higher-pitched, some lower. I wish I was one of those people who can identify birds from their songs. The crows and seagulls are easy enough, of course, their cries are so common and well-known, but the other cheeps and chirps and chirrups could be anything. Mostly though, my soundscape is the cars on the nearby main roads, the bleep of the pedestrian crossing, and the smatterings of conversations from people walking past, mixed in with the sound of rustling branches as they're caught by the breeze.

I always thought this was such a quiet, peaceful road. Near the main road, yes, but set away from the traffic with the brooding cemetery and only a few houses, so we've never had to deal with speeding cars or excessive numbers of people. But sitting out here, on a cold, dry winter's day, it's anything but peaceful. The birds are so loud, though not actually particularly close. I can see what looks like a sparrow in Next Door's tree, and another unidentified bird on the roof over the road is yelling its head off. I can see some birds hopping about in the giant hebe too, but they're too quick for me to be able to tell what they are. A coal tit flies up to the hanging fatballs, its high-pitched call repeated two or three times. Overall there's a veritable cacophony of different rhythms and pitches, and I find it hard to separate them out or concentrate on one at a time. I expected this exercise in noticing to be mainly about describing what I can see in front of me, but right now I can hardly look at anything because the different rhythms and sounds of the birds are so overwhelming and tricky to identify.

Sometimes I watch the activity in the garden from indoors, through the front window. An occupational hazard of garden-watching is that your very presence puts off many of the garden's regular visitors from showing up at all, preferring to wait until the coast is clear and then playing and eating and flirting and surviving in peace. Watching from indoors, it's not long before there's a ton of activity, with birds coming and going, uninhibited and undistracted by my presence.

But it's clear that this is not the whole experience. Being separate from the sounds and smells and temperatures and textures makes the visual spectacle abstract and removed, even though it's only on the other side of the window a few feet away. I make notes about the sparrows hopping and plopping about in the bush, the comings and goings on the bird feeder, the blackbird and robin trading places on a prominent hebe branch, then zooming across the garden to shelter under the cotoneaster when a group of children walk past on the pavement. But it feels like I'm writing one of those shots of text explaining the action in a silent film from a hundred years ago. I don't think I'll be doing lots of observation from indoors—suburbia feels unnatural enough, without hiding myself away even more from basic elements and sensations.

Heading towards the end of the month, we're being overrun by workmen digging up the road right outside the house and garden—laying down new gas pipes, I think. So to the usual background traffic hum, with its regular bass drones from enthusiastic accelerators, is added the racket of reversing vans, beep-beep-beeps, engine revs, juddering pneumatic drills, and shouting, all drowning out the sounds of the birds and the breeze. I hate that noise, it's become all that I can hear, and the birds are keeping their distance. More man-made 'improvements' divorcing us even further from nature. Even in my vaguely (if scrappily) manicured garden, watching nature these last few weeks has shown me just how full of life it is, but this incessant noise drowns it all out. It also occurs to me that, although I've lived in towns and cities my entire life, I've never really noticed this background noise before, and I've always managed to zone it out somehow. But now that I've noticed it, it's like I'll never be able to get rid of it—it constantly needles and demands my attention and just never goes away.

I've always had January pegged as grey and dreich. To be fair, it often is. But the colours in this place... If you'd asked me before this year about the colours in the garden in January, I'd have said mucky green and muddy brown, and grey overhead, but oh my goodness! Up till now, I would have said the sparrow hedge was completely bare, just stems and twigs. Now that I've bothered to look close up, it's actually dotted with tiny blobs of youthful lime-green proto-leaf buds, vividly contrasting with the more sombre dark greens of the waxy-leaved bush and cotoneaster. And the waxy-leaved bush itself has berries, bright red against the deep dark green of the leaves, a welcome splash of colour amongst the gloomy green and brown surrounding it. I honestly can't remember if that bush has ever had berries before, or if I've just not bothered to look or notice before.

Elsewhere, the heather by the front step, below the clematis, has new red and yellow leaf bursts highlighting the green foliage, particularly at the part of the plant nearest the wall. I wonder why some bits of the plant have different colours when it's all just the one plant? Who knew plain old heather could be so varied?

Even the grass on the lawn has turned out to be much more interesting than I've ever given it credit for. Below the bird feeder there's a weird clump of bright green grass, obviously different to the rest of the grass. A couple of months ago a delivery driver dumped a parcel just behind the feeder, underneath the conifer in the corner, presumably thinking it was more sheltered there than by the door, and he'd bumped into the feeder and knocked out a load of the seeds onto the ground. We didn't bother picking them up, partly because it was wet and muddy (the ideal place to leave a parcel, then), but mostly because we assumed the birds would hoover them up. I'm glad they didn't get all of them though, that clump looks much healthier and more vigorous than the rest of the lawn!

Although the lawn is only tiny, right from when we moved here there have been several varieties of grass growing together and looking a bit out of place. There's ivy creeping along and mixing with the grass too, and near the house is a clump of thicker, faster-growing grass. Along the edges of the beds and round the compost bin it grows long and stalky, where it's harder to reach with the mower. Moss is starting to move through a lot of it. I don't mind that, it gives it much more colour and character than a monochrome lawn—or, god forbid, that hideous fake grass that so many people are going for these days. I don't suppose we'll win any awards for it any time soon though.

There's some new life emerging, even in January. A couple of years ago, during the Beast from the East storm that dumped a load of snow on most of the UK, the cordyline I'd planted a few years before had snapped under the weight of the snow. I'd put the snapped off bit in the garden waste bin, but the stump of it I'd left, assuming it would rot down eventually and return to the soil. That was mainly laziness, to be honest, and not having anything else to put in there. But I've noticed not one but two baby cordylines emerging from next to the stump, and am pleased to see new life emerging despite my neglect.

The variations in light and colour saturation are infinitely more varied than I've ever realised before. One day the sky is a mass of grey clouds through which the sun tries (and mostly fails) to burn through, but then all of a sudden it'll be a pale, washed-out blue. With the thin, wispy white clouds it looks almost like a blue wash put down before the painter adds the depths of colour and detail. I've always said nowhere does blue sky like Scotland, but I usually mean those piercing Saltire blue summer skies. This pale blue, which we'll all have seen a million times before, feels brand new. And in the evening, the darkening blue becomes more dreamy, and the dark silhouette of the hebe branches and leaves against it yells out to be noticed.

I'd also have told you, if you'd asked about the garden before I started to actively look at what was there, that unless there's a howling gale going on it's pretty still. But it turns out I would have been wrong about that too. Looking up at the giant hebe, I can see just the very tips of the branches moving almost imperceptibly with the faintest of breaths. Of course I can't hear its breath like I can hear my own, but I know that even with last year's dead blooms still hanging on, it is teeming with life, and right at this very moment is getting on with the simple yet hugely complex job of surviving to see another summer.

The sparrow hedge too I often see shuddering—not the gentle breathing movements like when it's caught by a breeze, but jerks and judders which indicate there must be some birds hopping about in there somewhere. And sometimes a sparrow or three will suddenly whizz past my head from behind, so close I can feel the breath of their wings.

The cotoneaster, so much chunkier and thicker than the other bushes, is often more still. Having such a thick trunk and branches means it doesn't bend to the light breezes which brush the other garden plants. Its healthy and shiny green leaves show there's plenty of life going on there though, despite its outer stillness. It carries the promise of life to come, as in late spring and summer it is always mobbed by bees seemingly deranged by its potent, tiny flowers. Here in January, though, it is still, brooding benevolently, standing firm as it watches over the tiny world of this garden. I like the sound of benevolent brooding. Maybe that's what this project is all about for me too.

One thing about being in a garden this small, and this close to the street, is that I feel so self-conscious. Partly because I know I look a bit weird. How many other people are sitting out on their own in their front garden on a camping chair at the start of January? Plus because it's so small, and only takes a few steps to walk the entire length of it, I'm aware of how much of the garden is being taken up by me. I feel out of proportion, like Gulliver in Lilliput. What will the neighbours think?

As well as self-conscious, I also feel insecure in my utter lack of knowledge about this place. I can't name the birds that come to check out the feeders. Tit? Finch? Note to self: bring the bird book out here next time. Several of the bigger plants could be anything. The names I've given to some of the plants (sparrow hedge, waxy-leaved bush, etc) are meaningful to me, but I'm aware that it would be hard for anyone else to picture them if I can't give them their real name.

Names are such weird things. Ultimately a random collection of letters that form random sounds, yet when they're known they convey such meaning and reminiscences, a sense of legitimacy and belonging, at least to us. The plants and birds of course have no idea that we call them ivy or sparrow or rose or seagull, so the meaning and sense of belonging and legitimacy that we get from knowing is just a one-sided construct, nothing more. But sitting in the garden barely able to identify anything beyond ivy, rose and sparrow, I feel, not stupid exactly, but not quite belonging. It's an unsettling feeling. I want to know who and what I'm sharing this space with; I want to know it intimately and familiarly, rather than feel like Jackie No-Clue.

There are some garden secrets I do know though, and I feel a lovely conspiratorial buzz as I see them reappear each year. The clematis, as always this time of year, looks completely dead. No leaves, old woody stems, last year's remains coiling round the old faithful thick stems. But I know it'll only be a few weeks more and the leaf buds will appear, followed by hundreds of pregnant bulging buds waiting to burst into pink flower. I always prefer the promise of the buds to the actuality of the flowers, lovely as they and their burst of colour are too. Watching them fill out and start to bulge, the anticipation of spring and new life is exhilarating. It gets me every year.

February

This month is starting wet and cold, and I'm feeling self-conscious as I've dragged myself out into the rain, wrapped up awkwardly in waterproofs and trying to look natural as I sit on my camping chair under the umbrella, hoping that none of the neighbours will notice. Looking at the garden from beneath an umbrella is an unexpectedly strange experience—I hadn't realised how accustomed I'd become, in just a few short weeks, to the sky overhead as an integral part of my experience of the garden. The tops of the tall plants too—conifer, hebe, clematis—have suddenly disappeared behind the canvas dome of the umbrella, and my world has shrunk. I can hear bird cheeps in the background, but the predominant sound is the drip of rain on my hood and umbrella. New rhythms to add to the increasingly familiar patterns of birdsong.

There's a visible lack of birds. Up to now, I'd thought they were getting used to me, and weren't particularly bothered by my presence. My umbrella isn't bright, but it is patterned, and so is new and unfamiliar to them. Never mind—this is Scotland, so I'm sure they'll have plenty of opportunities to get used to it.

The plants react in different ways to the rain. The bushes with waxy leaves—hebe, cotoneaster, and waxy-leaved bush—look healthy and invigorated as though they're freshening up in the shower. The grass though, and the more delicate, thinner-stemmed plants, just look bedraggled and flattened: a look I'm definitely starting to emulate the longer I'm out here in the rain! The fallen leaves and flowers covering the lawn in a soggy mulch only add to the squelchy ambience. Times like this, it's hard to believe we'll ever see summer, so I need to remind myself often to look for hints—slivers of blue sky, dots of leaf buds—to remind myself that there will be a way out of the gloom. The garden might, right now, be various shades of mucky greens and browns, but the colour will come.

Storm Ciara is the first of the year's named storms to make its presence felt here. The day before was still, but I knew the plants and bird feeders, gently wafting in the breeze, were in for a battering. Sure enough, a couple of days later and here I am, sitting out in the tail end of the storm, which is howling around menacing the garden and anyone daft enough to be outside. One of the bird feeders, hanging from an upper branch of the hebe, is swinging about like a hammer round the athlete's head before flying off on its epic trajectory. In the calm moments between gusts, intrepid birds come and snatch a feed. What is this angry weather like for them? I can imagine it would be terrifying for a tiny wee thing, but then I'm a fair-weather purveyor of the outdoors, usually, whereas dealing with these conditions is probably hard-wired into them.

It's been a day of contrasts. Despite the wind and earlier rain, the sun is out. The bits of the sky I can see are a gorgeous blue, and the clouds are mostly fluffy and white—even the grey clouds aren't looking particularly malevolent. That wind, though! Against this fluffy, pleasant backdrop, it's howling through the street, the bushes are waving about madly, and with the volume and intensity of the wind I wouldn't be surprised to see Dorothy's house fly past in black and white, pursued by the Wicked Witch of the West.

Even the cotoneaster, normally so solid and brooding, shudders as one big mass. The sturdy trunk and branches aren't for snapping, or even moving much, but when a decent gust hits it, it judders not as individual branches but as a single entity.

The following week and it's Storm Dennis' turn. As with Ciara, while waiting for Dennis the atmosphere seems brooding and subdued, but heavy rain soon heralds the full force of his arrival. When I go out into the garden I'm forced to write through a hair haze, my hair blown every which way despite my being wrapped up like Michelin Man. The twiggy heathers on either side of the front steps are waving about furiously—I wonder if these suburban plants still retain the primeval knowledge of the exposed moorlands, where they'd be used to some brutal weather.

It's not all wind and rain though, even if it feels like it! On occasion the sun makes an appearance. Not feeble and pathetic, but enough to make me turn away from the unaccustomed brightness and revel in the blessed sensation of real warmth, even if right now it is still intermittent. The sun is high enough to pierce through the hebe canopy, dappling the ground and my notebook with playful shadows and hope.

The roadworks that so annoyed me in January haven't gone away. Now that the hole in the road has got progressively deeper, it's surrounded by metal fencing which clangs and clatters in the wind. Weird metallic music. If it was tuneful it would be reminiscent of Wintergatan or Steve Reich, but the atonal spangs and clanks are other-worldly and unsettling, if not menacing.

Later on in the month and the workmen have moved round the corner, so although the sound is still there it's more of a hum, the drilling and digging less piercing than when they were just a few feet away, and the ground no longer vibrating beneath my feet. I can hear the sparrows again, calling to each other as they hop about in the bushes and pluck up the courage to visit the feeders despite me being nearby. Alongside them I can hear the reassuring bongs from the bell of the nearby clock tower—man-made noise that I find comforting rather than annoying, thus shattering any Earth Mother credentials I might think I have.

The traffic noise is still there though: buses and cars humming along the main road. There's a superfast broadband van parked outside, so they'll be digging up the pavement soon as they lay cables throughout the city. I'm starting to think what I'm craving most, more than rurality per se, is some proper peace and quiet, where I can mainly hear birds, wind, rain or sea, rather than this constant thrumming of engines. Once it gets through my defences, it doesn't ever seem to go away.

It might be cold and noisy, but there are still signs of hope, even this early in the year. I've just spotted some white dots on the end of the ceanothus branches. Even in a month of brooding and waiting, life is not only pottering along but is pregnant with new possibilities. The leaves on the hedge are getting bigger and more obvious, there's no missing them now. And the red leaves on the rose, like new raw skin, are starting to unfurl and sunbathe—nothing wrong with a bit of basking as we start to pull away from winter. One stem of the rose has grown a bit taller and is starting to mingle with the straggly honeysuckle. I love this blurring of boundaries.

I spotted my first leaf buds on the clematis, and am over the moon! Along with the crocuses in the park down the road, and a handful of snowdrops I've noticed in people's gardens, I'm beginning to think spring really is starting to break through. Winter's not ready to give up just yet, and there's snow and ice still forecast, but I'm feeling hopeful. The bulk of the clematis, all thick and woody, seems to move as one in the wind, like the cotoneaster the other day. I was initially worried that I could only see leaf buds on the extremities of new growth that I'd not pruned last year, but now I can see all the old gnarly joints of the main woody bit starting to swell. It looks painful and arthritic, but that's the sign of life bulging just below the surface. It won't be long before the wood is covered and seething with new growth.

The honeysuckle, which I'd thought the other day was bare in the middle, also has clusters of leaves opening out, checking out the world after a long sleep with no cover. The bushiest, most mature leaves and branches are right at the top, a legacy of me never having bothered to prune it—I might have to give it a bit of a haircut, give the lower down leaves a chance to see the sun and bulk out a bit. Meanwhile, the jasmine's still looking pretty twiggy. It's fooled me before into thinking it's dead, then bursting into new life with those gorgeous green and yellow leaves. These always make up for the disappointment of the flowers, which never amount to much. I hope it has another lease of life this year and entwines with the honeysuckle—what with that and the rose starting to shoot up, there's the hope and possibility of an array of different colours, woven together in a glorious tapestry.

The hebe looks strong and vigorous with the piercing blue sky as background, and the ivy amongst it is filling in the gaps with a deep green that sings with vibrancy and colour as the sun sneaks into the garden to work its magic. Meanwhile, the leaves on the sparrow hedge are fair bursting out now. It won't be long before I can't see the sparrows hopping about in there anymore, which presumably will be when nesting and egg-laying begins in earnest. There are more cold snaps and possible storms forecast, so I hope the sunny days don't fool them into getting too frisky too soon.

One of my random childhood memories is of hearing a cooing from what I always assumed were doves: 'Trr trrrr trrrr, trr trr!' Every time I hear it I'm transported back to those moments standing at my childhood bedroom window, trying to see the beautiful white bird making this plaintive cry. I can hear it again now, in the garden, and for a moment I'm excited about the thought of nearby doves. It's wishful thinking though—a cursory glance at the internet (many years off and unable to search during my 1970s childhood!) shows that this is the call of our resident wood pigeons. Realistically, let's face it, doves are probably a bit posh to hang out with the likes of me.

The wood pigeons, on the other hand, are all too willing to let us know they're hanging around. Unlike the sparrows, they don't seem bothered by me at all. One has just flown low over my head—no other bird visitors (or residents, as I should probably more accurately call them) flap their wings with that much force. I'm a bit worried they might be nesting up in our gutter, as I often see them from the front upstairs window landing just out of view. I wouldn't be so bothered if they were the more socially acceptable swallows or swifts nesting there, but I'm less keen on the thought of pigeons making themselves at home. I guess London hasn't completely left my system, even after all these years, with this not particularly rational dislike of pigeons who are, after all, just trying to get by and live their lives the same as the rest of us. This feeling of animosity is bothering me a bit—aren't those of us wanting to get closer to nature meant to love it all equally, from microbe to giant oak? Pesky prejudices, getting in the way of Earth Mother pretensions (while I'm at it, don't get me started on rhododendrons). I guess I'm more of a work in progress than I'd sometimes like to admit.

I've come out here at lunchtime to try and avoid the workmen's noise—there's a bit of shouting, but mostly they're at lunch and the diggers are silent and still. It's actually really sunny and quite warm, shadows are dancing over my page and I'm having to turn my head away from the blinding sunlight. What a difference that makes—to the concentration of the blue sky, to the feeling of warmth on my body, and to the lifting of my mood. I'm still wrapped up in my winter coat, but the edge has definitely gone from the temperature. The lawn is mostly green, and the new leaves getting bigger every day on the bare sparrow bush are a vibrant lime colour, in contrast to the dark green big waxy leaves next to them. There are lots of hints of life waiting to burst out and celebrate the sheer wonder of existence. For now, I'm mostly having to take comfort from the hints, but soon enough I won't know where to look first as more and more new life jumps out to greet the world.

Soon I might start pulling up some of the dead bits—old crocosmia leaves, old achillea stems, and the straggly bits of grass in the flower beds. That's a losing battle, but I'll keep fighting it so the heather and ground cover don't get completely swamped. The pruning and pulling up of stuff, mowing the lawn even, makes me think of summer coming, and my mood starts to lighten thanks to the glimpses of sun and increased chatter of the birds.

March

I've resurrected our old bird feeder and hung it up with some nuts on the hebe. If past experience is anything to go by, it will take the birds a while to suss it out, but hopefully it'll be a little bit of extra sustenance for them as they start nesting and breeding again. The sparrows are flitting about in the hedge and tree, occasionally braving the hefty breeze of the tail-end of Storm Jorge to fly as far as the hebe. I've also seen them hopping about at the bottom of the bird feeder. They'll be beautifully sheltered in their hedge. The stems are nice and tight-knit, and now the leaves are starting to bulk out, it'll be less draughty. In the tree and shrub by the feeder it's a bit more precarious, with branches more susceptible to the wind. The tree still manages to always look graceful as it's buffeted about, but I don't think I'd want to perch in it today! We seem to be getting a storm every weekend at the moment. It would be nice to sit out here on a Sunday and not worry about my notebook (or my actual self) blowing away. I know spring is definitely on the way, but Jorge's tailwinds are doing their best to delay it a little longer.

I finally got round to making some more fatballs, and love watching the birds having a go at them. They seem to not be eating the seeds since I hung a tray onto the feeder to catch the spilt seeds—I might take that off and see if it makes a difference and if they return to it.

And something that has absolutely gladdened my heart and made me smile is that I've just noticed that Next Door has put up a bird feeder too and hung it on the buddleia, and there are sparrows going for it right now while I'm too close to our feeder. So the singing hedge[1] will hopefully be full of very close and deafening cheeps before too long! Wouldn't it be brilliant to have nests in both our hedge and Next Door's?

Another thing that gladdens my heart is watching the sparrows hopping and jumping about in the hedge, it's amazing how they can fly from inside there to the underside of the cotoneaster when it's so very tightly packed with twigs and branches. It must be amazing to be that agile. Of course, it's eminently ordinary to them.

A couple of the sparrows just came a bit closer to me. I really don't want them to get tame, but I'm

---

1. Whenever I walk past next door's hedge I am assailed by loud and frantic and joyful chirps. There always seems to be such a lot of activity going on in there—it's evergreen so I can't see anything, but oh, the sound! I've called it the singing hedge for years.

glad they don't see me as a huge threat. And now a gaggle of sparrows have landed in the hebe—I'm so glad we have that as another good shelter for them. If I stay still (or more preferably for them, just go away!) they might come in for a feed.

There's just a slight breeze, so the hebe, clematis and honeysuckle are hardly moving. Apart from the outer stray stems, the clematis in particular seems still. It's deceptive though, and it makes me glad that underneath that woody, cracked, dead-looking exterior, life is pulsing through the veins and waiting to burst out for its annual 'look at me' show.

The underside of the cotoneaster looks unwelcoming, with its thick, low-lying trunk and branches latticing together in a spiky cage. But I know the birds are in there all the time, hiding or checking out what's going on in the garden. There are more old chopped branches down there than I'd noticed before, and the grass is starting to creep in. Another small stem of holly has appeared which, along with the creeping bramble, offers them even more protection. There's a longer, spindlier bit of holly closer to the house which is leaning out—I don't remember it being there when we moved in, and only noticed it a few years ago. I wonder how they got there?

Exciting garden news, which gets me every year—I have now spotted the first clematis flower buds emerging with the leaves. It's still bare and woody, and I wonder if there will be as much growth as last year. Hopefully it will prove me wrong! Those little embryonic buds in their clusters always give me so much hope, and right now doubly so, with all this worry in the news about coronavirus and Brexit. There's talk of self-isolation and social containment, I think life is certainly going to look different for a few weeks,[2] but these beautiful birds and flowers can't be contained, they're carrying on and doing me the power of good.

I'm so, so excited by those tiny clematis buds. I'm not at all sure that it will be as extensively flowering as previous years—there are lots of swollen joints that don't look like they're budding, as well as the ones that are. But those tiny orbs of burgeoning beauty still fill me with hope, even if this year it doesn't turn out to be as prolific as usual. Right now (mid-month) the flower buds are two to three millimetres in diameter, just emerging from the base of the only recently-emerged leaves. The newest ones still cluster tightly together, but the woody stem closest to the front door has a couple of bunches that are starting to stretch out. As they get older they'll bulge more and more, like hundreds of pregnant bellies, stretching their skin in anticipation of that bursting forth of new, joyful life. It doesn't matter how crap I feel, it never fails to make my heart leap.

---

2. Footnote from the future: Oh my sweet summer child, how naïve you were! But thinking that life would change for a few weeks was probably how we got through it at the time. 'Just a few more weeks!'

Taking a closer look at the stem joints, it looks like more of them than I initially realised have a leaf cluster getting ready to emerge from their rheumatic cocoon. Some of them still look lifeless, but joints on either side are already budding, so I hope that although they're taking their time they'll peep out soon too.

The leaves that have emerged already look so tender, like they'd wither at the slightest cold snap. I guess all new living things—flora, fauna, human—are so vulnerable when they first emerge, even though they're growing stronger and more vigorous every day. Looking back to the rose, the leaves, which a few weeks ago made me think of raw flesh, look much tougher and stronger now, even though they're still pretty red. I hope the greenfly don't find them this year.

Turning round to look at the rest of the garden, it's like every single leaf and blade of grass is drinking in the sunlight, and almost glowing. Is it my imagination, or is the ceanothus extending its branches even more? I hope so—that burst of blue in early summer always gives me such a big lift. Meanwhile the ivy has weird little flowers—a bit like miniscule grape bunches on the end of a stalk. As well as the colours, I feel like I'm noticing new shapes here for the first time too.

There's a burst of yellow through the stems of the sparrow hedge. Next Door's daffodils soaking up the sun—another quick sign of spring pushing ever stronger through the blurred edge of winter. The tree in Next Door's garden is budding too, at last—it won't be long before I'll hardly be able to see the lamppost next to it. That will give better shelter for the birds as well. I love watching them survey their territory from the tree, but it is a bit exposed for them till the leaves are fully open.

The far, dark corner of my garden, under the conifer behind the bird feeder, looks like a cosy den. I'll leave it for the birds, but in these trying times a little, quiet, dark refuge in the fresh air sounds so very appealing.

The noise of roadworks is still going on and on and on. I know it has to be done, and will hopefully be over soon, but I feel like I'm forgetting what it's like to relax and enjoy the birdsong because of all the engine noise relentlessly drowning it out. I can see the cars, vans, lorries and buses thundering past on the main road. I always felt this was quite a peaceful and quiet place to live, but the constant coming and going of vehicles, and the incessant traffic hum, is changing my perception. The dream of somehow getting away from all this noise won't settle down.

On days where there aren't diggers and massive engine noise, I am so much more aware of the birdsong—trills and cheeps and chirps, and some chattering coming from the depths of the cotoneaster. I can hear gulls and crows overhead too, but none of them are drowning out the joyful, urgent chatter of the smaller birds, thankfully. Listening to that song in the fresh air, the busy birds calling out to each other, singing and yelling and generally bustling about their business, it feels like I'm drinking from the freshest spring.

I can't believe how blessed and 'light' I feel watching the birds going about their business. Never mind the anxieties of the day—pandemic, inept politicians, the rise of the right-wing, the climate emergency (an altogether terrible and terrifying combination), watching these small lives go on regardless lets me know that something bigger than all of us is still soldiering on, despite humanity's best attempts to stifle it. The toilet brush bush has lots of dots of green leaf buds, and the sparrow hedge is really leafing out now too, showing me once again how nature carries on regardless of all the inadequate political and administrative systems we've put in place.

HD is having to self-isolate (cold symptoms, I don't think it's covid[3]), and although I know he'll be working still, I can't help being envious that all he'll have to do all week is just turn his head to look out of the window, and he'll see this little micro-world waking up and bursting into life.

A week later, and the world is just weird. The country is not so gradually shutting down, schools are closing in a few days so I'll mostly be home schooling, I'll also be back working on the ward which I'm dreading, and everyone is tense and

---

3. This was in the days before home covid testing was available. His subsequent months of deranged tastebuds suggest my guess was probably wrong.

unsure. We'll only be allowed out once a day for exercise or food/medicine shopping. Only key workers like me will go to their workplaces.

Even the birds feel subdued. I should try and soak up a bit of sun, like the plants in the garden—it's hard to quiet my mind enough to look and notice, but taking some deep breaths of fresh air will hopefully help me to slow down, calm down, appreciate the stillness for a few minutes before going back into headless chicken mode. I hope this time of enforced physical isolation causes us all to slow down, breathe more fully and deeply, not just for the duration of any lockdown, but beyond it into healthier working and living practices.

I owe this to my family, to DreamGirl especially. I think seeking out these sanctuaries in the garden will be so important for both of us. I hope she can get the same sense of tranquillity that I find here.

It's the end of the month, and I'm out in the garden with DreamGirl, we're sitting in our camping chairs drinking in a little bit of sun, because of course the sun is out now that we're on lockdown and have to stay mostly indoors. Also randomly (and also fantastically—Scotland, you are brilliant), somebody appears to be playing bagpipes, fortunately far enough away that it's not too overpowering. DreamGirl just asked me if I like writing out here, and when I said yes she said that this garden is my 'calm place,' which is exactly right. My mind is buzzing, and I'm struggling to not feel anxious, but I always do calm down out here. Eventually.

Of course, I might be the one out here trying to actively notice everything, but today I had to cede the prize for excellent noticing skills to my lovely six-year-old, who cut through my pretensions and summed up everything I'm doing. It's not often I want to be a little kid again, but if I could have her way with words, I'd be delighted! Here's a couple of examples:

DreamGirl: 'I actually didn't notice how calming it was out here. I thought outside was a busy place with all the cars. I didn't realise you could sit out here in your chair, it's actually quite calming.'

DreamGirl: 'Mum, did you even realise we had a floor bit of the thing?[4] I never noticed before.'

Me: 'What else can you notice?'

DreamGirl: 'That one's up, and that one's down.[5] I've never noticed because I never looked before. And look, that bush has more leaves.'

I'll have to bring DreamGirl out here more often! Even though I love being out here on my own it is so good for her to look and see too. We're talking about making a bee hotel which is a great idea, as I think a lot of the bees which like the cotoneaster are ground/tunnel-nesting rather than hive-dwelling. That would be a brilliant addition to

---

4. She meant that the ivy was creeping along the ground as well as growing vertically.

5. The honeysuckle is climbing high up, and the clematis is leaning forward and down because of its weight.

the garden—I'd love half an acre to get creative and natural, but even in just a few square metres there's so much we can do. Talking of the bees, I'm already starting to see a few early ones scouting out the place, including a humungous bumblebee checking out the clematis. Come back when the flowers are open! There's plenty for you all!

APRIL

The start of the month and it's nippier out, I think we're due a cold snap. But although it's windy, it's dry, and whilst I'm wrapped up to the nines I'm enjoying the benevolent blue sky and delicate wispy clouds. DreamGirl's bubbles floating over the garden add more beauty, and the background traffic hum is joined by the flapping plastic covers of Next Door's mini-greenhouse. Now that's the kind of man-made noise I don't mind, people getting back to basics and growing their own. The wind is picking up a bit, it's amazing how something so unseen can make its presence felt so powerfully. Like the dastardly coronavirus, but also like the birds, who make up in melody and volume and energy what they lack in size.

Another day, and it's cooler, having rained overnight, and the sky is a uniform off-white. Overcast, but at least it's not foreboding. Most of the colour in the garden comes from the wet glistening shiny leaves—vibrant greens of new leaves on the ivy, hebe, sparrow hedge, and toilet brush bush, deeper and darker on the more mature ivy, cotoneaster, holly, and the waxy-leaved bush next to the sparrow hedge. There's an incredible aural colour too from the birdsong—an absolute frenzy of singing, activity, feeding, building, and (hopefully) reproducing. And the post-downpour smell is so refreshing and joyful!

I've started to notice how the weather can impact my mood quite significantly. After the exhilaration of a day or two of sun, and colours, and obvious pulsating life, a cold day can leave me feeling quite subdued and wanting to hunker down, get warm, and emerge later with the flowers and vegetables and baby birds. Other times, when it's sunny, I feel like I am so much more open to everything around me. A couple of times around sundown I've noticed a golden light out here. The clock tower, which can be pretty grey and drab when it's cold and wet, austerely looming over the street, is bathed in a golden red glow which looks warm to touch, even this early in the year. Especially when the sun's out, Scotland really knows how to do colour. There's something about the dense colour saturation which is so inviting, warm and welcoming, drawing you in ever deeper. Of course, in winter when everything feels like a drab, wet monochrome, you wonder what on earth drew you here, but the payoff in the emerging spring and the full summer gloaming is well worth the months of waiting.

I'm still struggling with external noise—loud motorbike noise, Next Door talking, DreamGirl leaping around—I have to be careful though not to regard this as just 'my' calm place. DreamGirl especially needs this place as much as I do. And of course none of us have as strong a claim on it as the birds, busy nesting and full of the urge to thrive and survive.

The hum of the traffic remains ever-present, and I've even started to hear the sound of trains approaching or leaving the station. We're too far away to hear that normally, so I guess it must be pretty still, relative to usual—or I'm just being even more sensitive than usual to all that noise. A small private plane flies overhead. Since lockdown started, I don't think I've seen a commercial plane in our particular patch of sky, which I like to think stretches from just behind the church, over the street, over the park to the housing beyond. I can't say I miss the planes, and I'd love there to be fewer cars too!

Sometimes, when it's not too cold, HD has the two front windows open and I can hear his music while I'm sitting in the garden. Somehow that's a happy rather than an annoying sound—partly because the birds are still much louder, but also maybe because the open windows signify a blurring of the boundaries between 'inside' and 'outside.' Yes, we're encroaching outside a bit, but we're also opening up so the inside can touch us with its warmth. Or coolness, depending on how perimenopausal I feel!

The leaf buds on Next Door's tree are filling out, pale white-green blobs against a light grey cloud. The tree beyond the church hall is budding too, but only just—I think it will look wintry and bare a while longer. HD has sown some mushroom spawn under the hedge and conifer in our garden—I wouldn't be surprised if the birds snaffle it all up before it becomes mushrooms, but it's another experiment and we'll see how it goes.

The clematis buds are getting bigger every day and the leaves are opening out so it's not looking quite so bare, although I still think it's a bit balder than last year. With a bit of sun, though, all the leaves on every single plant in the garden look like they're thrumming with life. I can see some new crocosmia leaves poking through the ground now, and the other day (stupidly, confusingly early) when I was walking past the garden in the street from the car I saw some red berries on the pyracantha. They're supposed to have white flowers in summer and berries in the autumn, so who knows what's going on there?

The cotoneaster leaves are glowing in the sunlight—I imagine them drinking in the sun to store it for the colder, duller days. Just on this one bush is a whole spectrum of greens—dark, light, reddish, variegated, in sun and in shadow. I can't wait to see it writhing with bees in a couple of months.

On sunny days I'm enjoying seeing the shadow of the leaves and branches dancing on the page, and wish I was better at drawing. Better though to remember it than try to recreate it, although I'll try to snap a photo of the effect. It's like the natural world reminding me that I'm a part of this too—I'm not just outside looking in, there's beauty that can touch me too.

What I appreciate right now is simply sitting here in my calm place, watching the natural world go by, thankful for the plants and creatures teaching and soothing me as they just get on with their lives, pretty much oblivious to me and my sporadic appearances in their patch. I'm noticing all sorts of things out here. The cordyline, which I thought had died after being flattened by snow from the Beast from the East storm a couple of years ago and then recently spawned a juvenile next to it, is now two juvenile cordylines side by side. I suppose I could think of something pseudo-profound to write about death providing space for new life and growth (which is something I do find quite abstractly inspiring, without wanting to diminish the raw grief of bereavement). But now, I just want to smile and marvel at nature's ongoing ability to surprise and delight, even as it's just doing what we know it always does.

The clematis flowers are opening, slowly at first before the onslaught of pink blousiness. The buds that are still not quite open are bunched together like a gaggle of animals—meerkats, maybe—emerging from their burrows. And the blue flowers at the foot of the rose are opening out too. I'm so glad I planted them, I just wish I could remember what they're called! Although the different greens in the garden are lovely, it's always nice to have dots of other colours. The ceanothus buds are pink and growing as well, I can't wait for them to open out into that perfect, glorious blue.

DreamGirl wishes the roses would come back, which prompted me to have a look, and I've spotted a couple of very tiny rosebuds, so that will be a welcome splash of flamboyant red later in the year. There are buds appearing on the allium mony too. I hardly know where to look first, it's all bursting forth in every direction.

The coal tit and its mate are calling—four single pitch notes, a simple four crotchet rhythm. There's something else trilling in the tree, I think I can see one of the blackbirds, and a couple of sparrows there too. Even though it's cold and getting blustery there's still so much activity going on, I can't write fast enough to get it all down! A crow caws nearby, a coal tit flits over to the feeders for a drink, and occasional snippets of conversation from people out on their state-mandated daily walk also float by. I was worried that the beanpole frame for DreamGirl's den, which HD constructed for her the other day, was putting the birds off, but if it was they've got over it.

It looks, from the tray that I put underneath the seed feeder to catch the spilt seeds, that there is one type of seed that they're not so keen on. Maybe I'll collect them up and use them for the next lot of fatballs—waste not want not! Of course, literally as soon as I wrote that, one of our blackbirds (the female, I think) has perched herself in the tray and is scoffing those very self-same seeds. I guess the seed feeder is probably a bit too small for the slightly bigger birds like the blackbirds, so the tray makes a great feeding station for them. She's scarfing the seeds down, so there we are—I'll leave them for the bigger birds.

I attended an online nature writing workshop as part of an online literature festival, and wrote my first ever haiku, about the bird feeders:

Trills, cheeps and squabbles,
Flapping wings and rushing breeze,
Tap against branches.
I'm quite pleased with that for a first attempt!

I think I'm going to have to invest in an app to identify all this birdsong, as the current lot singing away are mostly out of sight. There's a high-pitched urgent-sounding one, which might be the sparrow on top of our little tree, contrasting in tone with the laid-back blackbird who was just happily ignoring me and taking her time.

Sometimes I worry that me being out here is stressing the birds out, but I think they must feel safe enough because they are busy getting on with life. I can hear some loud sparrow squawks from the tree behind the feeder—I'm not sure if it's a squabble or a party, but it's pretty loud and raucous. Maybe they were just all yelling at me to put another fatball out already.

A gaggle of seagulls circle and chatter overhead, and yet again the trilling and peeping and squawking carries on all around: hebe to tree to Next Door's tree to overhead to back to the tree. The birds never seem to stop, but it's been a while since I've heard them at this massive volume and so many at once. There's an interesting stereo effect—one blackbird in front of me near the feeder, whilst another (its mate? I hope so!) is chirping away in Next Door's tree. The blackbird's song sounds calm and measured, unlike the sparrows squawking away in Next Door's garden on the other side. Completely different moods in each ear, and a loud single cheep right in front of me to make me jump!

Elsewhere, a couple of sparrows in the tree squawk away to each other—it's like they're responding to each other with perfunctory call and response chirps. For some reason it's reminded me of the Chuckle Brothers—I can just picture them barking 'to me,' 'to you' as they build their nest! I wonder what it will be like here later in the year when this frenzy of breeding and nest-building and chick-raising is over?

A blackbird carrying a white feather in its beak looks like it's wearing a false moustache as a cunning disguise, although of course it is presumably going to use it in nest lining. And then a sparrow flies in carrying something in its beak—I can't quite make it out to start with, but as the bird lands on the feeder it drops its cargo and I see it's a cigarette butt. I feel so sad—I'm so glad the birds feel safe and are settling here, they're doing their thing, excitedly picking up materials for their nests, but humans are ballsing it up, as usual.

By the gate, a ladybird sits basking in the sun on a shiny fresh ivy leaf, the red of the ladybird highlighted beautifully against the vibrant green of the ivy. I hope it's not an invasive Harlequin—I'm not an expert so can't tell for sure, but I'll hope it's not and enjoy nature's artistry.

There have been a few big bumblebees sauntering along just above ground level, their reassuring buzz a welcome change to the traffic din. If the birds were less squawky and a bit more melodic right now I'd say it was almost reflective of bagpipes, the birds' melody over the drone of the bees. Of course, plenty would say that squawking is the perfect description of bagpipes; I couldn't possibly comment!

I've also seen the bumblebees hovering and brooding over the ivy carpet like the Spirit over the waters. I wonder if the ivy pollen is available to them? I remember pruning the ivy last year, and the clouds of pollen released every time I cut into it, but if you leave it alone you'd have no idea the pollen is even there.

Another buzzing creature—not a bee, a hoverfly, maybe—is hovering above the sparrow hedge, then shooting upwards suddenly before returning. Although I can't see the actual wing movement, the superfast whirr of the blurred wings is visible against the blue sky. All that effort just to stay in one place!

I'm still trying to slow down and take in all this life and activity in the garden. Whenever I'm working on the ward (which is always heavy and anxiety-inducing), or trying to encourage DreamGirl in her home learning (which is more often than not stressful and distressing for us both), this postage stamp view is my call to calm. Life here is carrying on regardless, and I'm loving having the time and space and opportunity to actively notice it. I want to make some more fatballs, a very therapeutic activity, because I want to help this life carry on, and contribute to the hope and the sense of mental and physical grounding it's giving me.

It's Easter Saturday, and although people are still largely following social distancing regulations, there is a lot of background noise—people over the road working in their front garden, and loads of traffic. Who are these people and where is so urgent that they have to drive there? The pushing back against the strict guidelines is stressing me out.

The garden is still a haven though, and a good place to gather my thoughts. Our lovely next door neighbour died last weekend (not of covid), and so it's definitely the end of an era, since she and her husband moved here with their family in the 1970s, not very long after these houses were built. She's someone else for whom this street, this tiny strip of neighbouring gardens, was home, just like it is for me, though we've only been here a fraction of the time. There's a nice little community feel to this bit of the street, people are friendly without being overbearing, and it does feel safe. And above us all, the clock tower looms in my peripheral vision, the cockerel on the weathervane indifferent to the birds wheeling about around and below it, and unmoved by the pulsating frenzy of life and activity, and the mourning of a life well lived. I do like that clock tower, it's such an unusual feature to see from such an otherwise small and innocuous garden, and is such a solid, steadfast, reassuring presence in turbulent times. It's close enough for us to call it 'our clock!', and we always know we're close to home when we first see it at the end of a long journey.

I can hear some traffic, and in the distance what sounds like hedge trimmers, as well as the breeze bouncing through the leaves. Other than the movement of branches and leaves in the wind, though, and the occasional bird hopping between hebe and tree, it's come to a standstill in the garden. I know that's deceptive, and below the surface of the leaves and bark and earth there's tons of activity—sap rising, microscopic creatures doing whatever it is they do, worms tilling the soil—but that's a view I can only see in my imagination, despite its reality. I suppose that's pretty reflective of our lives at the moment in lockdown—everything seems to have stopped, but behind closed doors, in corridors of power, in hospitals and care homes, life (and death) is carrying on, mostly unseen.

I need to remember it's OK to hide for a season, to breathe and rest rather than try to fill the days with constant activity.

Up until now I've tried to ration my coronavirus-related news, to try and maintain my sanity, but last night a piece on Sky News about some NHS workers asked to reuse PPE made me feel so angry and despairing. My NHS colleagues are dying unnecessarily through a shortage of PPE, but apparently the answer is to discard basic infection control principles rather than properly manage the PPE shortage. So I need this calm place more than ever now—I'm honestly more scared about UK government incompetence (and lack of care, but especially the utter incompetence) than I am about the virus.

There's so little I can do—I already vote in a way that cannot ever support the Tories (much good it did this time round on the national level), and work on the ward with my own job on hold—so I must do what I can. What I can do right now is refill the feeders and the water for the birds, tend the plants, and notice what is going on as life beyond the garden postage stamp descends into more and more chaos. It's refreshing to spend time with the beautiful birds, as they go about their business oblivious to my worries about virus and home schooling and work and useless politicians.

I feel sleepy and lethargic during this lockdown—struggling to concentrate on writing or reading, despairing of home schooling. Primarily my inadequacy as an educator for a young child, but also worrying about DreamGirl and the effects this might have on her learning and development and mental health. For the first time since this all started I even have a little cry—only for a couple of minutes, but it feels good to let it out and open up the pressure valve a little bit. I missed a few days sitting in the garden, and it was starting to show—within ten minutes of being out again I feel calmer, more grounded, able to breathe more deeply and slowly.

As we reach the end of the month I've started to notice odd groups of people not socially distancing as carefully as they had been—I know we're getting a bit fed up (understatement) but I'd rather keep things strict for another few weeks than let things slip and see more infections again. The noise of the cars is louder than it's been for a while, so I think there are more people out and about. The weather is obviously influencing this behaviour, so in a way I'll be glad to see it cloud over a bit, if it keeps people indoors a bit longer.

Lockdown must be affecting me more than I realised. This home is my haven, I'm not stressed out about being here, and I love having it to come back to after a heavy shift at work. And this garden is of course an extension of that, my little bit of home in the fresh air.

I wonder though how lockdown is changing what 'home' means to me. To us all, really.

Unlike some people I don't feel trapped here in this place, although I find the cycle of news oppressive and feel more trapped by circumstances and politics. My lack of control over what's happening in the world is upsetting, disempowering, leaving me feeling like I'm floundering, but here at home, in the garden, the fact that I'm not in control of the plants and birds and growth and life is refreshing, and helps me feel more fully 'me,' even though I'm just an observer.

I don't have to be 'in control' of my life and destiny to be 'home.' It just needs to be where I rest.

MAY

I'm enjoying the warmth of the sunny front step on my behind! The sky is the most piercing blue I've seen it yet this year, it's glorious. The contrasts in the colours are breath-taking, I think because of the sheer intensity of the blue sky. The unpruned top stems of the sparrow bush are dancing in the breeze, the red tinge of their not-quite-mature green set off against the blue of the sky. The sky looks like it's been painted on by a computer programme, there's not even a single pixel of contrasting white cloud or paler blue. In contrast, the palette of greens beneath it run the gauntlet of the colour spectrum, the red of the spiny young rose leaves contrasting with the yellowy-green new leaves on the ivy and sparrow bush. Red and green pair together quite a lot in the garden—rose, sparrow bush, heather, cotoneaster—and yellow and green too, in the hebe and heather, as well as the scrappy contrasts on the lawn.

Even the paving slabs at the bottom of the front steps, seemingly grey and functional, are interesting at this time of year. Despite all our efforts to fill in the gaps between the slabs with gravel, the plant life of course was not suppressed for long, and sturdy-looking grass is peeking out from the gravel, as well as a more dainty-looking miniature dandelion. Although it is looking pretty scrappy, I like how the plants are so tenacious they'll grow in the least hospitable places, staking their claim to survival. I like how they break up the dark grey and browns of the slabs and gravel, and also how the lawn and the ground ivy won't be confined to their allocated place, but are trying to encroach, softening the man-made edges. Having said that though, I did cut back the ivy quite a bit on the pavement side of the wall, and hopefully stopped the hebe and pyracantha from being completely smothered. It has opened up the view a bit so made the garden slightly less private, but I think the balance is better now.

As well as the rooted plants on the slabs, there are blades of mown grass and dead bits from last year's clematis. It doesn't look like the birds are going to use any of it in their nests now, so I suppose I should sweep them up, but I'm not going to rush. I like a bit of imperfection. But honestly—I could do without quite so much bird crap on the ground!

The waxy-leaved bush has white buds, alongside the handful of red berries still hanging on since winter. Just like I couldn't remember if I'd seen the berries before this year, I honestly can't remember if I've seen this bush flower or not before. Maybe it has and I've just not noticed (or not remembered noticing), or maybe this is the first time it's flowered?

Maybe I'll recognise the flowers if and when they open.

Lots of yellow leaves are falling from the hebe now—DreamGirl pointed out how many there were. There's also new growth of course at the tips of the branches, and I can see how the branches end up getting so long and spindly. I wonder if there's a way of pruning it to encourage it to bush out in the middle rather than just at the ends of branches? Something else to research, although I suspect in this case after many years of no pruning (other than the branches hanging over the street that were starting to clonk passers-by on the head) we may have left it too late. There's no sign yet of the short-lived but always welcome new flowers—they're always my sign that, whatever else is going on in the world, and indeed in the weather, summer's definitely here. But it's not here yet!

Having said that, though, Next Door's tree is now covered in mature frondy leaves and tight clusters of white flowers. Just a few weeks ago, it barely had a leaf bud to its name. From this distance, the new growth reminds me of giant cow parsley. So for that to appear in such abundance in only a few weeks is a lovely sign of nature still doing her thing, and summer on the way.

The cotoneaster flowers—tiny pink discs—are still opening up. I can almost see them turning towards the sun and drinking it in. They also seem to stretch out hopefully to welcome the bees, although there are none on them yet. With a slightly stronger breeze, the leaves and branches of the hebe and sparrow hedge gently undulate like waves. The cotoneaster though stands a silent and still guard, only its outer fronds wobbling slightly while a falling clematis petal floats by.

The scent of the clematis flowers, starting to drop their petals already, is very strong, although not yet that 'gone over,' slightly fermented smell that signals they're past their best. They are still putting on quite the show, so there will be colour by the door for a little while yet. And wonderfully, I've counted thirteen rose buds, which will hopefully mean a riot of red in a few weeks. I don't remember the rose bush ever having that many at once, before; it would have a few open while other buds hung on a bit longer, which meant that the rose usually had blooms for months and months before finally admitting winter is on its way and calming down for a rest. I'd like that this year too, of course, but if these first buds all flowered at once I won't complain!

Below the clematis, the ground-cover (a sedum? I can't remember) I planted a few years ago is thriving and spreading, bright green tiny stars of leaves joining the older, darker greens and reds. That's definitely one of my successes, a terrific natural way of providing some ground cover.

Clematis petals are starting to lie forlornly on the grass, like confetti left behind once the wedding party has moved on. The lawn, which recently has seemed a bit faded, is springing up to meet the light rain, and the green seems more vibrant even as I look at it. At my feet are some clover leaves, which I'd love if they spread through the lawn, as the bees seem to gorge on their flowers when they appear. They only seem to be skirting the edge next to the paving slabs right now, with some clusters in the middle of the lawn too, but here's hoping! I'm not sure what to do about the lawn—I want the clover to thrive and flower, but I don't want the long grass to irritate HD's hay fever. Maybe I'll give it a light mow, but if the clover looks about to flower give it a few weeks off.

I'm enjoying the blue of the flowers under the roses and the ceanothus, they're a nice contrast to the pink of the clematis and the greens of everything else. When I have a bigger garden, I think I'd like to plan colour to last as long as possible—hopefully that would attract a greater variety of insect and bird visitors too.

The allium is pretty close to opening up and giving the garden a welcome burst of yellow, so I think we'll soon have a good mix of colours, to contrast with the increasing pink confetti of shed clematis petals.

Next Door's tree's white blossom has also started to drop and turn brown—it was fleeting, but lovely while it lasted. The smell now that it's turning is less lovely, more yeasty and cloying. I already miss the beautiful scent of the flowers in their prime, but it's good to know they'll be back next year to brighten up the street again, both visually and olfactorily.

The branches of holly in front of the cotoneaster have some new leaves growing too—smaller, redder—and I remember again that so many of the new leaves I've seen this year start off a rawer red before embracing their inherent greenness. There are greenflies on the holly leaf nearest to me, and I can see some of the leaves have been chomped at—I'm tempted to give it a spray of washing up water, but we've seen quite a few ladybirds in the garden this year so hopefully they'll get their chance to feast. Some of the rose leaves look a bit chewed and unhappy too, although that happens every year and it never seems to stop it from flowering beautifully.

I planted out a new lavender near the achillea, which was hard work as there was a big root (the cotoneaster, I think) very near the surface. But it was starting to wilt in its pot, so it was time. And already, despite being in full sunlight all day, it looks much perkier now its roots can spread out a bit.

The rose has started to head upwards, mixing more with the honeysuckle and jasmine, and the first of its buds is expanding like a balloon. It's nice to see a bit of colour there, as neither honeysuckle nor jasmine have ever been prolific flowerers, and every year I'm convinced the jasmine has finally breathed its last. But a handful of yellow-green stems and leaves are hanging on in there, helping to bulk out the head-level area that's more sparse, before the top-heavy honeysuckle finally bursts out into full growth. I must give it a trim though—I don't mind messy, but it would be nice if it would bulk out in the middle and not look so spindly.

Best of all, the new hebe flowers are now emerging. They've a while to go before they reach full size and give us their all too brief lilac gorgeousness, but I can't wait. Summer hasn't forgotten us after all.

A robin hops almost up to my feet, and I'm overjoyed as it's been several weeks since I last saw it. I'm glad it's still around. I want to say 'him' rather than 'it,' but have no idea if it's male or female. Cheeps, whistles, songs, trills—the sound of birds is all around at the moment. There are coal tits, sparrows and blackbird still visiting daily, never failing to be entertaining. The coal tits are going nuts at the feeder and fatball, although the sparrows are pretty forward about not waiting their turn—no British queueing up for these birds!

The frame of beanpoles which HD built as a temporary play den for DreamGirl is looking a bit forlorn now—we've seen sparrows and the (rather amorous) pigeons have a go at the string. I'm not sure if they don't like it or are just pulling it apart as a new fun challenge.

The branches of the tree behind the feeder shiver and shudder as the sparrows hop about on their business. Sometimes urgent, other times more calm and measured. This little community of birds seem to have such a sense of purpose which we've lost, thanks to covid. Of course, they have the usual survive and breed imperative, but even in the frenzied flitting from cotoneaster to hebe to feeder and all the variations of that route, it feels both purposeful and joyful. And I love that it's going on around me all the time—while I'm actively noticing it, but also when I'm oblivious.

It's highlighting differences too, of course—even I'm not so wedded to anthropomorphising everything I see them do and interpreting it through my own lens. While we're in lockdown we're restricted in our movements and much less physically active than usual, yet that contributes towards a growing sense of torpor and fatigue. The birds though seem to be on the go the entire time—singing, flapping, feeding, hopping, flitting, squabbling, it's non-stop. I can't believe that such tiny creatures have so much energy! It's not just the birds which migrate thousands of miles each year that are full of stamina—even the sparrows and tits and robins and blackbirds are just relentless, and they only have a range of a small street and its environs.

I could listen and watch out here all day at the moment. Just slowing down, slowing my breathing, watching this circus of acrobats and dancers and singers put on their show with no wish to self-promote beyond the imperative to breed. It's terribly cliched, but this time is such a privilege, and I hope it slows me down forever, and not just for this year of deliberate observation.

The monochrome blue of the sky is briefly broken up by a soaring, swooping white seagull. I wish it was an eagle or a red kite or something majestic like that, but here in suburbia we take what we can get! It was tiny against the clock tower, but its circles of soaring have widened so it appears much bigger as it floats directly over the garden. When it's not got its mouth open or squabbling over chips you could almost believe it was graceful.

That illusion of grace doesn't last long though, as another gull deposits a pungent 'splat' on the front steps, missing me by only a couple of inches.

Our male blackbird lands on the higher branches of the hebe, has a quick look round then flies off over Next Door's garden. I'd love to be able to follow where they go beyond the garden and see what they're up to. Even though I see them a lot and they're reasonably close when I'm sitting still, I don't have any kind of handle on their daily life, only the snippets of their lives that briefly intersect with mine.

A call and response set of single cheeps are breaking through the background hum of the traffic. One is from a sparrow in the hebe, the other I think towards the main road, somewhere in Next Door's garden. Meanwhile a little coal tit pecks around the base of the bird feeders, ignoring DreamGirl's abandoned flatbread in favour of the sparrows' discarded seeds. I watched the sparrows earlier from indoors—no wonder we're having to refill the feeder so often, they're so messy, digging about for whichever of the seeds they want and sending the rest flying. The tray below the feeder is quite full—I think I'll hold off refilling the feeder until they've eaten some of the seeds in the tray. They'll not go hungry—I'm pretty sure they're already the best-fed birds in Stirling! And a solitary blackbird joins the coal tit on the ground, having a go at the seeds. Its beak is yellow, its feathers a mottled black and dark brown—I don't think it's our usual male, who I'm sure is darker, but I'm a bit confused by its female or juvenile colouring but yellow beak. Yet another thing to look up and try and figure out!

And all of a sudden, a huge racket in Next Door's tree. A blackbird is yelling blue murder at a crow that had landed on the guttering of the church hall—I wonder if that's where the blackbirds are nesting, as it was not happy at all that the crow was so close.

Sparrows are hogging the feeder somewhat, and their behaviour is making me wonder if they're being a bit more territorial at the moment? It's a bit hard to tell but I think I saw an amorous male try his luck with a rather indifferent-looking female—although that could have been my imagination and it was just a bit of jostling for the same contested spot on the branch? Either way, they seem pretty active and vocal right now. Mostly there are four regular sparrows, but sometimes I spot six of them—I'm glad to see the word getting round about this garden as a good place to hang out!

I thought I saw a pied wagtail at the feeders, but that might be wishful thinking. They normally hang out on the pavement round the corner, hopping about near the pedestrian crossing, or in the supermarket car park over the road, but I've never before seen them in the garden. It was such a quick fleeting glance before it flew off though, chances are I was mistaken and it was a coal tit, but from that split second appearance it looked to me like it was smaller and differently marked. It's probably just my increasing enthusiasm for the birds and wanting even more species to find our little nook.

A young blackbird, beak mostly yellow, like it's only just started to mature, has just had a go at the fatball, standing on the water saucer to lunge at the fatball and taking quite the beakful while staring at me writing. I should move the water to the other side of the little platform, as I know birds standing on it like that to reach food are crapping into the water.

I can't believe it's taken me this long to think of that solution—lockdown has obviously made me even more sluggish than I realised!

Meanwhile, against a backdrop of bees buzzing in the cotoneaster and sounding like Formula 1 cars, a non-stop hum with seconds of louder roars as you get closer, the sparrows are singing—not just their usual chirping, but proper singing—and there's a more melodic song which I think is one of the blackbirds. I feel so lucky, like I'm listening to an orchestra. Accompaniment and virtuoso soloists!

A ragged looking tit (not sure if it was a coal tit or a blue tit, it was too quick for me) did a micro-refuelling at the feeders then headed back away. I gather they can look quite scrappy at this point in the year because they're working flat out to feed their chicks. I hope that's the reason for this one not looking quite as suited and booted as usual.

Now that the sparrow hedge is fully bushing out with mature leaves, I don't actually think the sparrows hang out there much anymore. Which is a shame, I'd love there to be a nest in there, although with the local cats around it does make sense for them to settle somewhere a bit higher up.

At the end of the month, I see a first from the window: a crow landing on the peanut feeder and having a good old go at it, rather than hanging out on the nearby rooftops or the clock tower like they usually do. I hope we see more of them, they're so beautiful and graceful, although I do wonder if more crows would mean the garden becomes a bit wilder, more 'tooth and claw'? Apparently though, although they would eat smaller birds should the opportunity present itself, they're not actively searching for prey, so I allow myself to hope that they will be able to co-exist in this spot. I'm also happy to see it going for the peanuts, as the smaller birds definitely seem to be showing a preference for the seeds and fatballs. The crow coming to the garden doesn't seem to have left any off-putting scent for the other birds—there's already a blue tit pecking away at the nuts quite happily, so let's see if this little ecosystem can accommodate even more species!

A bunch of sparrows arrive at the hebe, and they're inching forward till they pluck up the courage to fly closer to the feeders. I'm glad they're still wary of me. Much as I'd love to think I was communing with nature, they still need to be cautious and suspicious of humans. Sensible birds!

And as they start to hop around the base of the seed feeder, I feel like the universe is reminding me that life goes on despite me—a strangely comforting thought.

It's not just bird life becoming increasingly frenzied as spring moves inexorably towards summer. The insects and creepy-crawlies, particularly the bees, are out in force, and I'm amazed at how entertaining I find them.

I must admit to being one of those people with a definite hierarchy of invertebrates. Bees and butterflies are good, no question, whereas spiders, although they're good guys who eat household pests, are just too scuttly to not give me the creeps, and slugs can basically just go do one. Flies can sometimes be tolerable as long as they're not on my food, and not too numerous, and wasps I can put up with but wish they weren't such arses. And of course, midges are just beyond the pale. I think my default position is that for the most part the invertebrates are a good food source for birds, and of course we'd be screwed without them because so many of them are pollinators, but they've always been creatures of which I've struggled to become particularly fond.

I'm reading a book called *Dancing with Bees* by Brigit Strawbridge Howard, and hoping that I can catch some of her wonder and enthusiasm, not just for the cute fluffy bumbles, but also for the importance of insect life generally in our amazing world.

A few days ago DreamGirl spotted a ladybird on the paving slabs, and we watched it head to a cavernous gap between the slabs and the steps down towards the gate. She was worried it would fall and speculated it would have to fly to get across the gap (less than a centimetre), but instead it climbed up a blade of grass, crossed onto another leaf and carried on its merry way. I like that we're seeing ladybirds here, and that DreamGirl isn't scared of them. I hope we see many more.

I've started to see a solitary tree bumblebee on the ceanothus, and one time noticed the pollen pouches on her back legs, bright yellow against the black of her abdomen. It's not long before she's joined by another tree bumble and a hoverfly, and I watch the two bees working their way round the ceanothus flowerheads, in what looks like an entirely random order, at one point (despite the abundance of flowers) choosing the same one and bumping into each other! Luckily it didn't descend into a fight, and they regrouped onto separate flowers. They're so heavily laden that I can even see the pollen falling off them onto the ground. I'm overjoyed to be able to watch them work in such detail, what a privilege!

Another type of bee (I think) is hovering over the top edge of the sparrow bush and then over to check out the cotoneaster. This one is smaller, black on top with a dusty yellow underside. I'm so pleased that this tiny space can support not just the lovely bumbles, but so many other creatures. Before reading *Dancing with Bees,* I'd kind of fancied I could do my bit for the environment by getting hives and honeybees when we get the space, but now, thanks both to that book and through watching the bees coming and going here in the garden, I think the most important thing I can do is to introduce plants that are going to attract wild bees and other pollinators. And actually, I quite like that idea—not having the obvious hives and all the gear, but just encouraging the native bees to thrive unseen, with less fanfare and attention on myself.

Looking at the cotoneaster in the sunshine, I spot a tiny, delicate spider's web (thankfully for arachnophobic me, the spider appears to be elsewhere!). A couple of what look like dandelion seeds are trapped in it, but no flies yet. It's so fragile that it would be easy to miss—presumably for the flies too—yet it's such a beautiful piece of workmanship. From what I can make out, it's triangular rather than circular-edged, and I've just seen that it's alongside another even smaller web. It's so easy to spot the invertebrate life here when it's crawling with bumblebees, but there's so much more going on that I can only glimpse a fraction of it. As the breeze catches the web, I fear it will break, but of course it's better made than that, catching the wind and letting it pass through. And then all of a sudden, I realise the web does have its spider—almost imperceptible, it's incredible that this tiny creature could create such an intricate structure with a body like a pinprick and legs barely a millimetre long. She crochets the outer edges, expanding her lair, yet even though I'm right next to it I have to keep searching hard to see her, hidden in plain sight. And for the millionth time, I'm so very grateful to have this tiny spot to enjoy.

A mostly-black bee is exploring the ivy that's growing up the main trunk of the hebe. It's on a new ivy leaf, and seems to be vibrating itself, so I'm wondering if it's found a source of pollen there. I'm glad about that as it wasn't so long ago I chopped the ivy back a bit. I'm glad I didn't give it too severe a haircut!

There's a yellow and black stripy bee on the cotoneaster having a good old rootle around the pink flowers, many of which are now open. I wonder what the garden would be like with an insect's sense of smell? There's so much that as a human I'm just not experiencing, with all my senses—but I bet the mixture of smells is intoxicating. Same with vision: with our limited peripheral vision there must be so much that we miss all of the time, whereas a fly's psychedelic multiple simultaneous views must be amazing. Meanwhile the old faithful tree bumblebee is back on the ceanothus. What has happened to all the others, I wonder? Maybe most of last year's offspring didn't survive the winter, or something else happened?

I hope the bees that have visited the garden have picked up enough pollen and nectar to last them a few days, as the weather is going through a bit of a cold patch. I also hope they soon find the new lavender I bought to replace the one from last year that died in its pot.

Note to self: remember to actually plant this one out!

Towards the end of the month, my worries about the demise of the tree bumblebees turn out to be premature. Maybe they needed a couple of horrible weather days to make the conditions right for them to come out in greater numbers. Whatever, it's a joyous sight to see them crawling all over the cotoneaster, as well as one sunning itself for a few minutes on the white render of the house before returning to the lure of the pink flowers. There's a fly too, shimmering emerald green, checking out the cotoneaster. I guess they drink from flowers too, as well as scavenging random food. The sun on its green back gave it a piercing, reflective luminescence.

I wish the cars would pipe down a bit so I could better hear the bees' industrious humming. They're easy to see, clambering and flying from flower to flower, but the humming seems to complete the picture. Even though (as I understand it) tree bumblebees are a solitary species, these seem to be working well together, respecting the others' space and not muscling in, realising there's plenty there for them all. Would that we were so respectful and cooperative, instead (as our horrific politicians, especially in Westminster, are demonstrating again and again) of it being each for their own and sod everyone else.

Honing in to watch an individual bee, they don't look to my human eyes very efficient—the flowers are in clusters of three or four, and it seems to just collect from one flower in each cluster before moving to another bunch, which may be nearby, or may be further away on yet another part of the bush. But then, what do I know? I wonder if collecting pollen that way increases the efficiency of the pollination, so each individual cluster is potentially visited by several bees, rather than being drained just by one bee and then the cross-pollination is much more limited. I've no idea if that is correct, but it makes intuitive sense in a woo-woo nature's wisdom sort of way, at least to me.

At the moment, the bees seem to prefer the cotoneaster to the ceanothus, even though the latter's purple-blue flowers are at their brightest and finest. The cotoneaster flowers presumably pack much more of a punch in terms of the nectar and pollen they can chuck out, though they are much plainer and less showy. The bees keep coming back for more without seeming to deplete supplies in the slightest.

The bees (and what looks like a couple of wasps, though I can't be sure) really do sound quite frenzied and urgent, and I've nearly had a couple in my face as they dart and zoom about. The air is thick and treacly, and I wonder if they're gathering with extra urgency in case of worse weather later?

As usual, there's too much background noise—traffic and strimmers, mainly—and thanks to *Dancing with Bees* I've learnt a new word, 'anthropophony,' man-made noise. Plenty of that around here! There aren't as many cars as before lockdown, but these drivers surely aren't all key workers. I hope people don't let things relax too soon and undo all the good that's been done in 'flattening the curve' of the virus. I fear though that as people get more fed up they'll take more risks.

The birds are still making their aural presence felt though—the urgency of reproducing and feeding growing broods means that cheeps, whistles, songs and trills are all around. A lot of the bird chatter is very insistent, and even birds over the road can be heard as they yell at the top of their lungs. I wish I could experience and see the street how they do, just for a few minutes, see it through their perspective. The things that I barely notice must mean so many different things to them—shelter, home, food, danger, rivals—it would be fascinating.

As well as the birds, the sound of the wind is still there, despite us being on the verge of summer. It rushes through the trees beyond the church hall, and closer to home gives the hebe a good shaking. Another day and I unexpectedly hear the rush of water—the neighbours are filling their paddling pool. Too bad they'd notice if I took a quick dip! Plus their toddler wouldn't be too thrilled about sharing it with me, I'm sure. On a warm day though, the thought of sitting in a pool of water—however plastic and artificial the pool is—with my book and a cup of tea seems like the height of decadent luxury!

And amongst all the frenzy and constant traffic drone, the sonorous bongs from the clock tower provide a reassuring, 'grounding' sense of home. Even though it's man-made, the sound just feels right, and part of what's meant to be here, in this place. Which of course is absolutely correct, we as humankind are part of nature and the natural world, even as we royally cock it all up.

They've just announced a further three weeks of lockdown in Scotland. There are rumours things may start to relax a little in England soon. I'm not sure that's a good thing to do right now. I've taken next week off from working on the ward, and am so thankful I have this little patch of green to help ward off the blues. I think I might make it more of a reading spot too, and encourage DreamGirl out here more. I'm struggling with the guilt about her reluctance to do much in the way of home learning, and my reluctance to be more pushy. But guilt won't get us anywhere, and this calm place is a godsend and potential key to getting us all to chill out and remember what's really important.

I've just heard that a friend's partner has died. I only met him a couple of times, but he always seemed so full of life, and I'm just stunned at what's happened. But in the face of death, life in the garden is still going strong, not stopping or even pausing, not now. I can't help but think about how my friend's world will feel like it's completely stopped, while here in the garden there's constant feeding and flapping and yelling, new insect and bird arrivals, more and more flowers opening and bulging and providing food so that life can carry on. I'm thankful for the reminder, even though my heart's breaking for her, and I'm wanting to keep close to HD and DreamGirl. Life is precious.

My energy levels, unlike all the creatures in the garden, have never felt lower. I'm so sluggish, and many days I'm sleeping for a good few hours during the day as well as overnight. I'm missing my pre-lockdown morning swims, and feeling their lack on my energy levels and mood. The buzz of the bees and songs of the birds does go a long way to lifting the gloom for a short time, but I wish I didn't feel so tired all the time. However, I'm still grateful that this little patch of outdoors lets me reconnect and face the madness of lockdown life a bit longer. I'm craving more and more these moments of connection—not to think anything profound, just to feel the sun filtered through the hebe dance on my skin, hear the birds go about their business, watch the cotoneaster and hebe for bees, enjoy the activity on the bird feeders, watch the greening of the leaves and the bursting open of the buds, and just breathe in a bit of the outdoors. How could this be widened out into an experience for people who aren't lucky enough to even have a tiny patch of garden like this?

After a week of horrific racial violence in America (yet again), a Twitter book group has started up looking at nature writing from diverse perspectives. The first book is *Trace* by Lauret Savoy, and from the three-page prologue I'm already excited to read it. I'm part of the establishment demographic for so-called nature writing—basically, white and middle-class—and I desperately want to play my part in making nature, and nature writing, more inclusive. Another thread on Twitter asking about urban nature writing has provided another long list of books for my wishlist—the more I look, the more I can see there is already an abundance of written riches, but just like in nature, I think there's still room for more. Anything I write will probably be

'more' rather than particularly 'new,' but even still,
I hope my voice will be welcome to join in.

JUNE

H ere in the garden, during this extraordinary and constricting time, I can slow down, look at what's growing and which creatures are visiting or making their home here, and it gives me a sense of my place in the bigger world, even though the actual world here is tiny.

The bees are hovering over the cotoneaster, the bits of long grass in the scruffy flowerbed that evaded me the last time I tried to tidy up and pull out are nodding their seed heads in the breeze, and the rose is announcing more colour and blooms every day—four or five fully out, and another four or five close to opening out any day now. The hebe shoots are opening and letting even more flowers emerge, it'll be gorgeous in a few weeks. The allium is nearly fully open, adding a touch of bright buttercup yellow to the mix, just as the clematis has finally given up the last of its petals, the inner fluffy centres now bald and bereft but still standing to attention a wee bit longer. The clematis leaves just missing the shade show a slightly tanned hue in the sun, whilst the leaves in shade appear green and purple.

The waxy-leaved shrub has lost most of the white dots it had briefly last month, although there are still a couple of clusters of berries left from the winter. And the smelly bush looks like it has new flowers coming, so I'm happy about that—when they're here the scent is gorgeous and strong. Its leaves, glossy on top and matt underneath, same as the cotoneaster, look parched, but it's survived here longer than I have and will be here long after we've left.

A stripy bee still industriously works the cotoneaster flowers. More of the flower petals are looking browned, fewer of them still fully pink. I wonder if that means they're going over or if they'll be able to sustain the bees for a while longer. I hope so, I'm not ready for them to move on just yet!

We've started going to the area beyond the cemetery, near the main road, where there are some trees and the patch of ground underneath them is left wild and uncut. DreamGirl has started calling it the 'nature studio,' and there are tons of wild flowers and grasses, and lots of cuckoo spit. It's a lovely space for DreamGirl to explore the trees and play. I think they might be the trees where the blackbirds are nesting.

I've spotted a couple of clover flowers in the lawn, so hopefully the bees will find them soon. I did a rough mow, avoiding the clover and a pretty little tiny pink flower with fronded leaves. DreamGirl stood guard so I wouldn't cut it down. I'm not actually convinced our mower blades are sharp or low enough in any case, you still can't tell the grass has just been cut. Our visits to the nature studio have me wishing for a big enough garden that I can let the grass grow wild in at least a good chunk of it, but in this tiny spot it's still suburban enough to just look messy, rather than romantically natural, if it's not cut occasionally. Another clover flower nestles under the heather, out of the range of the lawnmower.

I love that there's still so much that I'd normally overlook in the garden that I'm able to notice in this year of slowing down.

By the end of the month, more clover appears. They look a bit bedraggled, but I hope the bees find them, especially since the nearby park, which had been left for ages and was a beautiful riot of clover, has just been freshly mown. At least the wet weather we're having, and which is forecast to continue into July, means I won't be mowing here any time soon.

Watching the hebe flowers emerge during June is always a delight. They start off spindly at the start of the month, reaching out like ET's finger, then soon develop just a hint of pink, the promise of more to come. They never let me down, never fail to cheer me up. I always know summer is here when they are out. By mid-month they are starting to open—this year I noticed one on the pavement side first, but soon they'll be rampaging all over. Even though they're fairly short-lived, they're faithful friends, back every year.

The lilac-coloured petals start to turn white and drop off soon enough, leaving the garden covered in their confetti again till next summer. As soon as the flowers are out, and even when they start to turn white and drop, the bees are all over them, I'm definitely going to have to cultivate another one of these if we ever move away. Once the flowers are over, I'm going to do a quite severe pavement-side prune, as the flowers are weighing down the branches and making passers-by duck.

I'd love to say 'well, let them duck,' but of course it's more important that disabled or visually-impaired people don't get caught up in them. I want this garden to be a joy, not something that gives people an unexpected fright.

The rose is on great form this month. Twelve or more flowers fully out, and more buds still to open. And a new shoot as well—a new stem covered in red, raw leaves, opposite another new stem I spotted a couple of weeks ago that is now covered in bright angry maroon spines. This rose is another one that always inspires me. It doesn't matter how damaged the leaves look, it's always pushing out new life and seemingly yelling 'look at me!' to the world. I'll have to think carefully about which bits to prune later on—it's a bit leggy and heavy at the front, so I might cut it back quite low to give it the chance to hopefully regroup and bush out a bit next year.

In the meantime, I deadhead the flowers that have gone over, in an attempt to lengthen the flowering of the others and encourage new buds, so we'll see how that goes. By the end of the month, after their glorious blousy show, they are starting to shed their petals. I feel a little melancholy watching them fade away on the lawn, curling up after giving so much short-lived beauty. But I'm grateful that I get to share the vibrancy and in-your-face-ness of the roses while they last. And even now, as the big blooms go over and shed their petals, there's a new bud appearing on a more spindly stem which I had thought about chopping. So that's given it a bit of a reprieve, and I'm happy that the flowering will be prolonged.

The heather by the rose has a handful of white dots—I'm glad my pruning of it earlier in the year didn't finish it off—and there are a few dots on the heather the other side of the steps too. Along with the allium in its bright yellow glory, and the ceanothus still bravely hanging on for a bit longer to its purply-blue flowers, I'm glad for all the colour still here. The honeysuckle too has a few more flowers, and one small one higher up that's properly opened. It's nowhere near as vigorous as the honeysuckle up the road, the other side of the church, but I'm glad for a sign that it's not yet giving up.

Also not giving up is the jasmine—no flowers, and every year I think I've killed it, but right now those yellow and green leaves and new stems are snaking their way through the balder bit of the honeysuckle, just above the rose, and that too makes me smile.

Down on the ground, the lavender now looks completely at home and established, and the achillea and blue flowers whose name I've forgotten, planted a couple of years ago, are also doing well. The blue flowers haven't had the best year, it's taking a while for them to recover from being walked on by the workmen who were doing the walls last year, but there are a few flowers, and it's starting to spread towards the cotoneaster, so hopefully next year we'll have another lovely blue carpet there. And the achillea, with its pale green ferny leaves, has flourished this year. No flowers yet, it's too early, but the leaves are vigorous and bursting with life. Hopefully it won't swamp the lavender, and there's space enough for them both.

The cotoneaster flowers are now definitely past their best, although a few heroic bees are still patrolling it to make sure they've not missed anything. The ceanothus is shedding its petals, although there's a fair bit of blue still there, but all attention soon will be on the hebe where this year's flowers are getting longer and more mature.

The branches of the toilet brush hedge and sparrow hedge are both getting long and scruffy, and could probably do with a cut, but if possible I want to wait for the toilet brush flowers to appear first. Some of the pavement-facing hebe branches are getting low and sticking out into the pavement space, but again I'll try and wait for the flowers to go over before cutting that back. The waxy-leaved bush next to the sparrow hedge is also showing new growth, as well as doggedly hanging on to a couple of berries from last winter. There are lighter green leaves at the end of the darker green branches, though the new leaves are just as big and waxy as the old ones, so they have probably been growing for a while without me spotting them. It's hard to get the balance right between encouraging new growth and cutting it back. I love the exuberance and scruffiness of it all, and certainly won't be going for the immaculately manicured look, but this is such a tiny space that I sometimes feel a bit pushed out, or like the garden is closing in on me like one of those old movies where the hero is stuck in a room where the walls and floor are closing in and threatening to squash them to oblivion.

A day of rain and all the colours in the garden seem even more vibrant. The raindrops are sitting, still whole, on all the leaves, flowers, and blades of grass. The lowest roses look drenched, but the other plants look like they're drinking it in as much as they can. The lavender is standing proud (hooray, I think I didn't kill it![1]) and a couple of stray, long blades of grass that have gone to seed in the same flower bed droop like willows over a river. I want to join them, bowing my head in the onslaught of such awful news in politics and health (virus, race protests, plus of course environmental and social degradation), and both lament and pay tribute to the good that I know is still around.

Mid-month, the achillea is sporting what looks like a couple of proto-cauliflowers—I think this must be where the flowers emerge from. There's also a glob of cuckoo spit there, which always used to gross me out, but now makes me happy to see nature continuing to do its sticky thing, and another creature finding a home in our garden.

A couple of weeks later, and the achillea is really going for it. I can't even count all the cauliflower buds, and buried behind the achillea's ferny leaves the lavender is looking healthy and thriving. The ceanothus is now over its flowers, but I hope it continues to grow—I'd be happy for it to take over a bit more of that corner. So would the bees, I'm sure! The hebe flowers are mostly out, and the yellow and black bee with the white bottom (a banded white-tail bumblebee, I discover later) is working its way through them. Even the spindly branches with

---

1. Footnote from the future: it turns out I was overly-optimistic, and the forthcoming winter finished it off.

just a couple of leaves on the very end have tiny flowers. The crocosmia leaves are growing up tall and strong too so we'll have a splash of red in a few weeks. I love how little splashes of colour appear at different times round the garden, as though the artist is filling in more details, dampening down others.

The holly is thriving too, the whitefly seem to have disappeared and the smaller leaves on the end are starting to lose their dark red and bulking out a bit. An ant (which I haven't seen much of in the garden this year, although I'm sure they're there) is walking all over it. I'm not sure there's much in the way of food for it now, but what do I know? I trust the ant to spot stuff that I'll definitely miss.

A sparrow perches on the old cordyline stump, checking out what seeds have fallen to the ground. There are a couple of sparrows—male and female, I think—hopping about behind the feeders, and a tit was flitting about the trees too. I couldn't see what sort, it was too quick for me! Both sparrows and tits are never far away, no sooner do I replenish the feeder than they're mooching about, checking it (and me) out.

We've seen a new bird on the peanut feeder, and think it might be a juvenile starling. I did wonder if it was a juvenile blackbird, but as the adults never seem to use the feeders but hop about on the ground, I suspect a starling is more likely. It had a go at the fatball earlier too—it jumped up out of nowhere, grabbed a huge chunk in its beak then fell to the ground without its feet ever making contact with the feeder, or its wings ever attempting to flap. Despite all the gloom of lockdown life, I know I can still smile, because that really made me laugh.

On a walk I saw a sparrow fly into a soffit (or was it a fascia? Who knows what they are anyway and what the difference is between them?) of a nearby house, so I bet there's a nest there too. I love how enterprising they are, finding such ingenious spots to safely bring up their young.

Back in the garden there's a right old cheeping match going on with several sparrows. There's one at the top of Next Door's tree, and I think at least one of the others is on Next Door's roof or the church hall roof. I've refilled the seeds and fatball, so hopefully the sparrows and tits will be along soon. Using peanuts instead of seeds in the fatballs to make them last longer didn't work at all, they're wolfing them down just as quickly as before. I've also added a quartered apple to the fatball feeder, rather than just chucking them in the compost, so we'll see how the birds take to them, or not. They seem to have finally discovered the peanuts, so hopefully this will give them a wee change and not upset their insides!

A gaggle of sparrows below the church hall gutter are yelling their heads off, flying into the gap. I bet that's where 'our' sparrows are nesting. There were four or five of them, and oh!—there's some hanky-panky going on right now! Surely a bit late, but maybe a second brood will appear?

DreamGirl is whistling at the birds. Whenever any of them move, she's convinced they're responding to her whistle. It's very sweet.

Towards the month end and such exciting news—we've seen three sparrow fledgelings near the feeder! My favourite thing is seeing them sitting next to each other on the branch in a row, like Sarah, Percy and Bill from *Owl Babies*. Guess what I've named them, although unlike their literary counterparts, if they were on their own I wouldn't be able to tell them apart. They're about the same size as the adults already, but their front especially is super-fluffy. Sometimes the adults will feed them beak to beak still; sometimes they have a go themselves, but they haven't mastered the feeder yet, and I've seen one of them chewing on leaves on the branch, wondering why it's not getting very far! Our other main visitor at the moment is one of the fat pigeons. I don't want to put up stuff to keep it away because it can't help being what it is, but it is hoovering up vast amounts of our seeds.

The apple experiment didn't work, so the apple quarters are now in the compost. I did put a bit down for the pigeons but even they weren't fussed by it!

Friend Cat (which is what DreamGirl calls the cat from over the road) is really well camouflaged at the foot of the feeders. I've just noticed it, but it might have been there for ages for all I know. DreamGirl has quite rightly suggested we stay in the garden so the fledglings don't attempt to come into the garden while the cat is here. I don't want it getting any ideas!

I'm noticing a huge amount of poo in the garden recently—the ground ivy is covered in white splats from the birds in the hebe, but also there are some brown ones on the grass which look like animal poo. Probably just the fat pigeons. I'd love us to have frogs or hedgehogs, which frankly can poo as much as they like. But the area is far too small for them to be viable.

After rain, the cotoneaster still has plenty of bees working it. I wonder if rain makes the flowers release more scent to attract them? Even though the flowers are going over now, there are still tree bumbles trying to eke out every last bit of nectar. I hope they have another source they love as much as this to keep them going. A giant bumblebee also just flew low over the garden, ending up in the cotoneaster as well—it must be twice the size of the tree bumbles and making such a racket! It was moving so fast it's hard to describe accurately, but was mostly black, with I think a dark yellow stripe to the abdomen and another to the thorax. The sound was the most striking thing though—a very low drone thundering through the garden. I wish I was better at identifying all these plants and animals and insects—what a townie I am, although I'm hopefully getting better at it.

Elsewhere, a bee on the hebe is working one length of flowers methodically before moving on to the next. Where do they nest? It wouldn't surprise me if it's somewhere near the nature studio, but I do know they can find all sorts of nooks and crannies. I'd love to be able to follow them back and see where they're starting from and returning to.

Both the under-feeder trays have what looks like slug or snail slime in them. I don't usually see either much during the day, but maybe they're chancing their luck when it's dark and they're less likely to be spotted by the birds? Or me? When I do see them though is after rain. I even got a picture recently of a snail's underside as it travelled across the front window, and I've seen others on the lawn and on the ground cover in front of the clematis, as well as the ones with the swirly pattern on their shells that hang around the clematis all the time anyway as soon as the leaves and flowers appear. I haven't seen any tiny baby snails yet—last year we spotted loads of what looked like individual bits of pale gravel stuck to the door, and when we looked closer they were actually perfect miniature snails. I don't think I'd mind them so much if they stayed that size!

HD and DreamGirl are off round the block for some exercise and fresh air, so I'm taking the opportunity to sit in the garden for a few minutes without having to play dinosaurs or fairies or whatever TV-knockoff roleplay she wants me to play next! It must be so hard for her. At six, she is aware of what's happening and why we have to stay home, but has such different needs to us in terms of socialisation and activity, and poor girl, we're her only source of non-electronic entertainment. It's hard enough for us. HD has to work so hard as several of his team are furloughed. I'm still tired and miserable after my couple of half-shifts on the ward each week. Goodness knows how my colleagues who actually do full shifts several times a week are still standing. It's brutal. I am struggling to balance making sure she's OK and carving out some time for myself, a lot of which ends up with me sleeping, I'm shattered. But I'm an adult, and can make (some) sense of what is happening. How can a six-year-old be expected to be unaffected by all this, especially one who doesn't have another child or children around to play with? I do fear for the longer-term impacts of this on children. I hope we can step up to being there for them when this does finally calm down.

What I can and must do is have her join me out here in the garden as much as she likes, and put a lid on my occasional irritation with her interruptions. I want her to enjoy it outside too, and see it as somewhere to relax and recharge and value and protect, just like I'm learning to.

Mind you, the peace isn't peaceful for long, even out here. Today I thought I'd have a nice sit down in the garden to contemplate the passing of another year (happy birthday to me!), but after months of peace, there's more drilling and digging going on—more broadband infrastructure work. I don't know how long they'll take, but I want my calm place back. With my feet on the lawn, I can feel the vibrations from the pneumatic drill on the pavement just a few feet away. If it wasn't so noisy it would be so beautiful—the ceanothus is starting to shed so the lawn underneath is flecked with blue confetti, and I can still see a few industrious tree bumblebees, but hearing them, even just a few centimetres away, is impossible.

The birds are sensibly staying away. I miss them. I'm sure this work is necessary, but I need them to hurry up, I just want to clamp my hands over my ears and pretend they're not there. No chance of that though—I try to look at the hebe flowers to cheer myself up, but I can't look at them without seeing the workmen and their hi-vis tabards, and hear their clattering and shouting.

Lockdown is hopefully going to ease down to the next phase soon. Part of me is hopeful, but also nervous—so much has changed these past few months, not all for the bad. I hope we carry on noticing, being thoughtful, angry about injustice, and in awe of the nature on our doorstep. I must admit though, I'm feeling weary, not just about lockdown, but also wondering why I'm bothering to dream about writing when there are so many incredibly talented writers already writing so much more beautifully and evocatively than I ever will. I'll get over it soon enough, I already know that the key is to just keep on writing anyway, exercising the creative muscle will hone and improve it. But today I'm fed up.

Other than a dark brown and white splattered blob that I'm honestly not sure if it's a poo or a dead slug, I'm not really seeing much new in the garden this time.

I think I'm even starting to feel tired of the work of noticing.

But I have to keep looking, as I know how enriched my life has been this year with these snatched moments of slowing down and seeing what's around me, realising how much I usually miss. I'm also slightly overwhelmed by the realisation that, for all I'm seeing and noticing and appreciating, I know there's so much more below the surface that I still have no idea about—underground creatures, fungal connections between plants, insects and maybe birds in the denser bushes, pests or hazards maybe hidden away too.

I worry about my own and my loved ones' health, during this time when we have so much time to worry—like the garden, for all we live with our bodies for years and know it, good and bad, better than anyone else, there will be stuff going on underneath that we have no clue about, including potentially sinister changes.

My thoughts are going dark, even whilst the garden in summer is mostly so bright and vibrant. I don't like that.

I'm glad to have this space to take my thoughts out of myself for a while.

JULY

A month of extremely changeable weather. One day I'm in waterproofs and hanging onto my brolly for dear life, the next day I'm hanging onto an ice lolly and soaking up the sun under glorious blue skies. The wind is never too far away either—even if it's fairly gentle at ground level, the noise of the wind in the trees beyond the church hall is loud, like waves lapping on the shore as the branches shiver and shake. I love that sound, it's like natural therapy, at least for me. And of course—this is Scotland, after all—often we have all of these things in one day. Blue sky with grey cloud, depending on which direction you face; bright sun with strong breeze; thick heavy air following thick heavy rain; even fluffy white clouds in the piercing blue sky while raindrops land on my bare arms. I never knew what 'all four seasons in one day' really meant till I moved here.

There's still plenty of bird activity going on. I'm convinced I saw a thrush at the foot of the feeders a few days ago. The tits aren't around much at the moment, and the blackbird only occasionally, it's almost exclusively the sparrows and the fat pigeons. I guess the bird I saw could have been one of the sparrows, but from the markings on the front it looked very much like a thrush to me. I hope that's not wishful thinking. I also spotted a lone coal tit and lone robin through the window—I wasn't sure if they were still about, but I'm glad they came and are still using the feeders.

The birdsong is nowhere near as frenzied as a couple of months ago, when they were all full of the joys of spring. I catch a new bird call, but can't see where it's coming from, so no hope of identifying the singer, sadly. It was a single note, sliding up in tone like a glissando. I can only see seagulls circling overhead though, and even I know it's not them! Other bird sounds are still also present—I catch a bit of something quite melodic, so hope the blackbirds are nearby, although I've not seen one for a while. The trr trrr trrr of the wood pigeons pierces the muggy air, and smatterings of cheeps and calls occasionally break through too.

I've been wondering some more about birdsong. It's pretty clear that each species can communicate with their own ('have sex with me,' 'predator alert,' 'here's some food,' etc), but I wonder if they can identify other species or even understand some of their utterances? In the same way that I would recognise someone speaking German or Polish or Japanese, even though I wouldn't know for the most part what they were actually saying. I think I'd like it if they did, that all these different birds aren't just in their own oblivious little bubbles looking out for number one, but aware of the others with whom they share their little patch. They'd probably make a better job of getting along and accepting difference than we are, to be honest.

I gather that this is the part of the year, once the intensity of nest-building and chick-rearing is over, that the birds start to get their new plumage. That would certainly explain the white fluffy feather at my foot, and the others dotted over the lawn.

The wood pigeons are really making their presence felt. There are frequent low flyovers, over our heads, so we know they're never far away. One of them entertains me by stepping about on top of the hedge. I'm sure it's trying to figure out if it can reach the feeder without me seeing it. The other one is patrolling the pavement and flying up to the top of the gate. I only need to cross and uncross my legs for them to fly off (or attempt to; I'm still mystified as to how they actually get off the ground, their attempts at flying are so laboured), but they're not far away, and every so often I can see the scruffier one's head peering at me over the top of the hedge.

We moved the fatball feeder slightly because the pigeons were sitting on the edge of the water tray to get at the fatballs and then crapping into the water, but they weren't fooled for a minute, and merely alter which branch they sit on to reach the food. I must admit I'm starting to develop a grudging respect for them. They're only doing what pigeons do, and no amount of human scheming will stop them! We took the tray off the post underneath the seed feeder to clean it, and while it was drying the sparrows dropped seeds onto the floor and the pigeons happily hoovered them up. So whilst having the tray has been good (or at least better) for the grass, maybe if we don't have it the pigeons will stick to ground foraging, which I don't object to. I am aware that these pigeons basically change my mindset from 'hug the trees, let's all be natural,' to 'Mrs UKIP we don't want your sort here,' and that is actually troubling me a lot. It's not dissimilar to how I feel about rhododendrons, but that's for another time.

While I'm getting angsty about whether I am inadvertently turning into Mrs Daily Mail, one of the pigeons has just landed really close and doesn't seem even remotely bothered that I'm here, the cheeky sod! It's been peering at me from the steps, and just sauntered up the steps to our front door while I watched! On top of that, HD just told me that all the time I've been watching that one, the other one has been sitting on the sparrow hedge watching me. They're definitely cleverer than I give them credit for, although I'm still not yet ready to accept our new pigeon overlords! I do appreciate that they're making me laugh though—this is a year which could do with some more comedy, frankly.

HD has built a new lowish roof for the bird table, to try and slow the pigeons down a bit and give the other birds a chance to eat without being pushed out. I'm sure they'll come up with a workaround soon enough, although this morning I did spot one of them in the feeder tray looking pretty disgruntled. I also saw one earlier from the window, standing on the roof and sliding down it in slow motion, looking extremely puzzled at this new experience. It won't take them long to work out how to muscle back in, and they're being so entertaining that I won't actually be too sad to see them succeed.

A bird which I thought previously was a thrush, but which I am now more convinced was a female sparrow, is pecking about at the base of the feeder, pretty well camouflaged in the muddy patch where a combination of dropped seeds, bird crap and incessant scratching and pecking has done for the grass. I know from last year that we'll see the sparrows all year. Let's hope the tits and blackbirds hang around too, though I've not seen any blackbirds for a few weeks.

I still fill the feeders in hope though. I think the feeding has slowed down. The fatballs seem to be lasting longer, so do the seeds, so we can probably slow down on the food for a while, until the realities of encroaching winter mean the birds need all the food they can get again. The birds haven't completely stopped feeding though—I've seen a jackdaw on the peanuts recently and the robin hanging around the seeds, and lots of juvenile sparrows are still about. I'm happy to see lots of bird life still going on—even while they're slowing down a bit, they're still around and seeking out the sustenance of this place.

One day I popped into the school playground to donate some too-small school uniforms to the uniform exchange project and pick up some bigger clothes. I saw two goldfinches there! Obviously we don't really see birds in the playground in normal times as it's full of children playing, and I've never seen finches in the garden here, but now I know they're not too far away, I'll live in hope that one day they might discover us!

More excitement another day when I look up while sitting on the front step and see a bird I've not seen before skim past. It looks swallow or swift shaped, but it is solitary so I'm not sure. I can't make out any markings, it's just dark against the background of the blue sky. A familiar flapping sound lets me know the pigeon hasn't gone too far and hasn't given up yet. I do admire their tenacity, even when I'd sooner see more of our other birds. It lands on next door's gate and peers at me from there. I look up and am rewarded by another glimpse of the swallow or swift careering about the sky. Even the pigeon can't take away my sense of excitement now!

Insect-related excitement comes at the start of the month, spotting a beautiful bright tortoiseshell butterfly on the hebe. I manage a rubbish photo (it was high up!), and hope we see more. I'm amazed it could find any free space on the hebe, which was covered in bumblebees and hoverflies.

Back from the park and there's a bumblebee on the paving slabs, not moving. I was going to bring it out a spoon of honey water, to help it get going again, but it's moved into the grass of its own accord and has been climbing blades of grass and clover ever since. I'm still not entirely convinced it's well and behaving normally, it's almost like it's forgotten how to fly, but it's working its way through the clover flowers so I shall trust it knows what it's doing.

The same bee has now wandered over quite quickly from the lawn, across the paving slabs, to one of the lowest-hanging hebe flowers, and it is working its way up that. I still don't think it looks right, I've not seen it fly for even a split second, but while it's drawing energy from what nature has provided I won't interfere. The contrast though in its movements compared to the other bees is quite striking. Just now it dropped down to the ground—not far, but it's not making any attempt to fly, and merely wanders over to a flower that is brushing the ground.

I'm not quite sure how to react to it. I could anthropomorphise its perseverance in the face of overwhelming odds, or be inspired by its dogged clinging on to life, or feel guilty at not intervening. And doing what, exactly? This is the sort of thing that makes me feel so inadequate and alien and apart from 'the natural world'—I know so little, understand even less, yet want to belong here and inspire others to care.

It's not unlike how I feel/felt at work, in research, in nursing, in academia—the dislocation, the sense of not fully knowing and being part of this particular place and time, the imposter syndrome, of course currently heightened by the uncertainty around the coronavirus. No wonder people are so stressed and anxious. Maybe that's the only lesson I can take from my bee: we can only do what we can do. But for all that, watching the bee, and being reminded of the Biblical care for the sparrow and the most seemingly insignificant of creatures, has given me hope and new understanding that every life, however dislocated or ordinary or boring, is of fundamental and intrinsic value.

Throughout the month I spot more tortoiseshell butterflies, but they remain coy to photos and defiantly shut their wings when I come near with my phone. The changeable weather is a worry, I hope they're OK and find somewhere to shelter. Another one zips past to Next Door, where the buddleia is starting to flower, so hopefully it will be covered in butterflies soon. Last year it was the painted ladies all over it (they had one of their ten year blooms, apparently, where they are much more numerous than usual years), and in previous years I've seen lots of peacock butterflies there. Maybe this year will be the year of the tortoiseshell?

The hebe seems to be where most of the insect action is this month. It's positively humming, there are so many bees working the flowers. I wonder what they'll move onto when the flowers go over? A stiff breeze blows through and gives the hebe quite a shake, and more petals come floating down to the ground, but the bees don't seem too bothered, they're still clinging on, urgently gorging and drinking while they still can. I guess, like nature all over, it's feast or famine. The feasts are transient each season, areas of plenty rarely last long. There's a ham-fisted lesson for our times if ever I saw one! Like the sun that peers out from behind the clouds (as it is doing right now), and we gratefully soak up and drink in in the rays because we know winter is coming, it must be the same with the insects and these flowers. I'm so happy we can host this feast, I wish it could be for longer. I know I'll miss them when the flowers are over for the year.

A couple of bumblebees I've not seen before, black all over apart from a ginger bottom[1], methodically work their way round each spear of flowers. I'm not sure if they're newly arrived or if I've just not noticed them before, or just glanced at them and assumed they're tree bumblebees. I hope they're not too scunnered by the falling temperature. They seem quite vigorous and energetic at the moment, and presumably have somewhere cosy nearby to shelter.

At the start of the month the hebe is heavily laden down with flowers. I first noticed on the pavement where previously I could pass under it, now it's in my face! Sitting out here the last few weeks I've heard several passers-by admiring it and saying how beautiful the flowers are. I have to admit that most of them have to duck as they walk underneath it, so I'm definitely going to have to cut it back a bit once the flowers have gone over. I hear the trunk creaking against the fence, presumably the flowers are weighing it down so much and making it lean more. It's not yet turning the air into that awful sickly-sweet rotten smell of flowers going over (Next Door's buddleia is the biggest culprit for that, later in the year), but I don't think it will be too long. The flowers are already shedding though,

---

1. I checked later – they were red-tailed bumblebees.

with the ivy, grass and paving covered in petal confetti, and the spears, so recently covered in delicate petals, bare or balding rapidly. When it starts turning white, this hebe always puts me in mind of Miss Havisham—impressive bridal blooms losing their sheen, but never their dignity. Even as the glory fades, it maintains its dignified and benevolent oversight of the garden.

Despite the shedding and creaking, though, the hebe stands tall and solid, and I feel reassured there is an established, mature presence in the garden while other plants still find their feet. This plant was here long before we were, and will hang around long after. I might be a relatively fleeting presence here, the newer plants my main 'trace' when we've gone, but ultimately this thing called nature will outlive us all. Notwithstanding humans' foolish attempts to subdue and pave over it.

A couple of random hebe shoots have appeared by the cordyline, and I'm not sure what to do about them. On the one hand I'd happily leave them to do their thing, but realistically this garden can't fit any more half-decent-sized shrubs, never mind a huge great thing like this! Plus if we move I'd love to be able to take some with us and have a go at growing something as impressive in the new place. But would it be better to let it grow where it is (where it's doing fine thank you very much), but then when it's time to try and dig it up find the roots are too widespread to go into a pot, or would digging the shoots up now be better for the roots, but then it has to risk over-wintering in a pot, where I have to admit I have a less than stellar past form with outdoor pot plants? I don't know—I just know that whilst we won't be here forever, I'd be heartbroken to leave all this behind, and if I could take even just a tiny trace of the garden with me it would make the moving on, the separation from this place, that little bit more bearable.

The achillea patiently waits its turn as the next focal point in the garden as far as newly opened flowers go. The clusters of flowers on the end of their poles are initially a deep burnished orangey-red before they become their mature yellow. I don't recall the bees being particularly into it last year, but I guess I'll find out soon! The lavender is still flowering too, although right now with the achillea on the ascendancy the lavender is getting a little swamped. Hopefully if it can establish itself it will grow and expand a bit next year.

Lower down the achillea stems I can see tiny blobs of white which look like new little proto-cauliflowers, same as the ones which have now turned into the red, orange and eventually yellow flowers. Maybe this means we'll get a second wave of these flowers too. Quite a few of the stems have open orange-yellow flowers now, currently visited by a fly (I want to say bluebottle, it's that sort of a fly, but smaller with a green rather than a blue sheen). The stems are leaning, as though the flowers are too heavy for them. I'm pleased with how the achillea has filled up that area beneath the window, and given some lovely shape as well as colour with those delicate ferny fronds.

The achillea isn't the only colour in the garden, of course. The magenta heather is starting to flower, and in the rain the other heather is showing a strong contrast between its brown stem and yellow-green leaves, as well as white proto-petals. I'm happy that every time it seems that one plant's flowers are fading or falling, elsewhere in the garden something else is picking up the baton and preparing for its own turn in the spotlight.

All the waxy-leaved plants are more vibrant and full of life and colour than ever. The raindrops glisten on the longer blades of grass, deepen the red of the remaining rose petals, and intensify all of the various greens. A snail sits under the windowsill, minding its own business—I'm sure they and the slugs will be enjoying this weather and abundance of flora, and I feel a bit mean that I'm hoping for a cold winter to finish them off naturally.

Checking out and photographing the white sedum flowers, I notice a tiny strawberry plant, complete with runners, growing in a crack in the paving slab! I don't know where that's come from, as we're not growing any strawberries. I think the most likely culprit is one of the birds, who must have eaten a strawberry somewhere then 'deposited' a seed where there was enough dirt for it to establish itself.

The sedum itself is going great guns too. The delicate white flowers have been out a few weeks, taking over from the allium which is fading and drying, but it's the ground cover I really love, dinky red and green leaf stars covering nearly all of the available ground, and starting to appear in some of the gaps in the brickwork which holds that bed up. Such a simple, tiny little plant, but it makes me smile to see how it's made itself at home.

The honeysuckle has some flowers, higher up, taking over from the current crop of roses which are now mostly over and which I've just dead-headed. There are just three blooms hanging on still. DreamGirl is sad when she sees there aren't many roses left, but perks up when I show her some new buds. And there are even a handful of jasmine flowers. The jasmine is never very prolific, but I'm happy to see (and smell) the few flowers that have appeared. And more new flowers are appearing on the smelly bush (actually choisya, but I've always called it smelly bush because of its gorgeously scented flowers), and also the fiery red of the crocosmias, easily glimpsed through the ceanothus and hebe leaves.

All these flowers mean the garden is a heady mix, and the smell starts to match the fuggy feeling of the air, attracting lots of flies. The whole place has a 'heading past its best and about to feel a bit manky' air about it, helped along by the ripeness of the compost bin, which is so pungent you can almost see the smell.

On the way to a play date, we walk past a small patch of grass with clover, buttercups and dandelions. DreamGirl spots a bee on a dandelion. She then asks me not to mow the lawn for a few weeks in case there are flowers our bees can feed on, and I must admit to bursting with pride. That's my girl! I'll balance it out with HD's hayfever, but that's a request I'm happy to oblige, if I can!

Behind the front window I can see our oak seedling, now twenty-one months old, about three inches high with four big leaves.

DreamGirl asks: 'Why are we growing an oak tree anyway?'

It's a good question, of course! We picked it up (along with a few others, but this was the only one that took) at Aberfoyle Forest Park in October 2018, the first school holidays after DreamGirl started school, and I must admit none of us thought it would last this long! We won't plant it in this garden as the space is far too small, but I'd love it if one day we had some land to plant it out and watch it grow. Failing that, there are oaks on the walk to Balquhidderock Wood, and in Plean Country Park, so if we're still in suburbia when it really needs planting out then maybe we could plant it there? I don't even know if you need to get permission for that or not. But as a native tree, I'd love to be able to plant it out to do its thing for the next several hundred years, long after we've gone.

The calls of the seagulls overhead make me feel a bit nervous. Mainly about being crapped on, to be honest. It reflects my nervousness about lockdown continuing to lift. People are trying to get back to normal, which is great, but I still don't feel quite right about it. I don't know if it's fear, exactly, just that this period of lockdown has exposed the paradox of feeling confined and stifled while also increasing my appreciation of the little bit of world around me. Caution is no bad thing, and I hope it also means being more thoughtful of ourselves and others. But seeing the Tories down south crowing about opening pubs while still insisting people visiting hospital for appointments can't be accompanied, and having inpatients unable to have any visitors, plus people moaning about having to wear a mask still, makes me feel judgy, angry, and despairing as much as I hope for a better future. On the ward we've had patients with us for weeks and months who would love a visitor, and families who would love to visit, but I guess they'll just have to go to the pub instead. It makes me so angry, it's all about money above all. I suppose all I can do is make sure that I and those around me are on the right side of history by encouraging kindness, care and concern over selfishness, ego and a 'me first' mentality.

This garden is the start for me, and my family, but it can't be the end.

Weirdly, the gate is open. Not weird in itself, but I have such a strong feeling of wanting to close it, so that I can be safe and cocooned in this space and not open to the outside. This is purely psychological, especially given it's a big iron gate with huge gaps so I can see straight through it into the street and passers-by can see also straight into the garden. It hardly closes us off to the world. But that feeling of needing not to be open to the outside is powerful. I guess it's an ongoing lockdown reaction, 'new normal' and all that, and reflective of the shrinking of all our worlds.

Another lockdown reaction, for me at least, is periods of mental and emotional lethargy, wanting to just hide and sleep and not think about anything. If I don't think about things, then I won't have to face them. It feels like I can't see anything new. I hope familiarity isn't breeding laziness at looking and noticing, and indifference to the beauty around me. That's the last thing I want. I'm enjoying the breather and the chance to slow down in the fresh air, though. That will be enough for now. Soon I'll finish up on the ward and return to my actual proper job, and feel both glad about returning to a normal routine, but also a little apprehensive at letting the wider world encroach again. I'm also over the moon about stopping work that I have really struggled with. Never mind 'NHS heroes,' I've been miserable and grumpy about my lack of choice and feel inadequate and deskilled and a burden to my colleagues. It's not even a fear of contagion that's worrying me, so much as over the last few months all our security has been in home and this small area around about us, and everything else is 'out there' and not in our control. And even though I've been off work for a couple of weeks, the hospital is definitely a place that feels 'out there' for me right now. I'm also worried that I'm losing the ability to think critically and innovatively (which is, I think, what got me the job in the first place), while I've been hunkering down in this little bubble of unreality. Sitting out here though has been so important, not just for my mental health and personal enjoyment, but also for little glimpses of 'out there' as I catch snippets of strangers' conversations, phone calls, arguments, and lives as they pass by.

It does worry me, not so much that we won't return exactly to how things were before lockdown, but that too many people will insist on 'back to normal.' I'm scared that 'business as usual' will be back too soon, without the necessary reflection on whether it was all good. It reminds me of the nostalgia for the communist era in parts of Eastern Europe. It wasn't perfect, but when you're stuck with the worst effects of rampant capitalism, the past is going to seem more rosy and even something to aspire to get back to.

The lawn is getting leggy and spindly, but it's a bit too damp to mow. Grasses by the edges of the lawn have visibly gone to seed, especially under the hebe and ceanothus. The various different types of grasses are getting tall, a bit straggly, and are starting to tipple over drunkenly.

I think 'slightly drunken' is a good description of my experience of the garden. The flowers as they bloom and then go over, leaving a slight trace of the scent of fermentation as they turn brown on the ground, remind me of having one too many beers—still basically doing OK, but not quite as in control as they perhaps could be—while the bees and wasps slurp on the hebe flowers in a bacchanalian gorge-fest. Likewise the slightly overgrown grasses, bits of hedge, ivy and hebe spilling out of their tidy gaps onto the lawn and pavement like reality TV stars spilling out of their limousines. I kind of like the not standing to attention-ness of it all, letting it all hang out and just being, but it's also maybe a little bit threatening—I don't have complete control over this growth and of all the life throbbing away at and under my feet, and trying to tame it could easily take away from the life and vitality of this patch. Any attempt to get this garden to walk along a straight line will end up with a trip or a wobble. So I choose to just enjoy the slightly tipsy life here—giggle in delight at the signs of life, blow the perfectly natural scheming of the fat pigeons to eat as much food as possible out of all proportion, and at the end of the day in a boozy glow declare this little glob of life, lust and laughter my best friend.

I do like that even at its tidiest, this garden is still on the slightly scruffy side. To me, that feels more welcoming and relaxing. The hebe confetti petals have bunched up on the edge of the paving slabs and have mostly turned brown now. I should probably brush them onto the lawn or onto the ground ivy so they have a chance to give back to the soil. I might not be able to see much beyond the grass and ivy above ground, but the thought of an abundance of tiny life below the surface is amazing. I wonder about the 'consciousness' of those microscopic life forms—how do they experience their environment, and its interactions with me? For all of their complete indifference and lack of knowledge of me, they surely experience something when I walk over them, drop skin flakes on them, and periodically mow the lawn above them.

Earlier, we saw Next Door with her mum and the new baby, and she was saying how her school friend had grown up in our house and expressed delight when she had recently come to visit the baby that the clematis in our garden was still there, as it was her dad who had planted it. I love that there's that living connection to the past, before we were here, and that even though I see it now as 'our' clematis, the roots in time go back beyond us. Plus of course, when we move on, our legacy too will be in the garden—some of the plants are ones that I've planted, plus hopefully the bird generations still finding shelter and sustenance after the glory years of our feeders.

I don't fully understand why I want to have a legacy here (of which this book will be part), but I know I want to tread deeply as well as softly, to be remembered in the environment as well as on the page.

AUGUST

One thing that surprised me moving to Scotland was how wet Augusts are. In my head, August is meant to be the sunny month—it certainly was growing up in England—so the ferocity and frequency of the rain in Glasgow was a shock to the system. Here in Stirling, not even forty miles up the road, but further east, heavy rain and spectacular storms are much less frequent, but August is still pretty sodden.

The thunder isn't often overpowering. The recent thunder sounded like someone was taking the bins out to the front of the house, rather than clashing celestial cymbals an inch above my head like the west coast storms. But at least it's done the trick of clearing the air. In the aftermath there's even a bit of blue sky, pale but trying valiantly to peek through mostly white cloud. And there's enough of a breeze that there aren't the hordes of insects that have been hovering miasmically over the flowers and grass the last few weeks.

Later in the month, and a heavier and more prolonged lot of rain has left bright white raindrops sitting on the blades of grass and clover leaves, lots of individual dots with some larger blobs like mercury, collecting and subsuming the nearby smaller balls of water till they're heavy enough to slide away. The still drops look like they're waiting in anticipation for, well, who knows what? Their joining with other globes of water, of course, or maybe waiting for the sun to evaporate them into the air? I don't know, but especially looking at the bigger rainwater globes lined up along the individual blades of grass, I sense hope and anticipation, further growth and life to come.

As is often the case after heavy rain, parts of the garden are looking bowed down, the achillea leaning drunkenly on the (not entirely sober and upright itself) holly, the roses are starting to shed a few petals, the smelly flowers are getting browner by the day, and the hebe branches look weighed down with the cares of the world. The rogue shoots of new clematis stems are bright and perky, as usual. I'm constantly chopping them off to stop it completely taking over the entire house. But within a few days of the last haircut, more shoots are eagerly and cheerfully pushing their way through for a piece of the limelight. It always makes me smile, even though I know I'm going to have to chop them back if I don't want to leave the house like a jungle explorer hacking my way through the vines.

Although there's not a nip in the air yet, there's less sun warmth and the day is starting to hint at autumn. Just as I remember spring and winter almost merging into and breaking through each other's boundaries earlier in the year, here's a reminder that the sunny warm days will be gone for a while soon. We visited Plean Country Park recently, and it's the first time this year that I fully registered the leaves in the trees starting to turn yellow. I was hoping to stay in denial about that a few weeks more! It's only very subtle, but it's definitely starting.

This weather means that I'm often adopting my favourite 'eccentric neighbour' pose—camping chair, waterproofs and brolly—and hope I finish writing before the postie comes. My main intellectual activity seems to be figuring out the best umbrella position to avoid drips on the notebook!

Sitting out in the rain, and once again the predominant sound is the pat pat pat of rain bouncing off the umbrella. The ivy leaves mostly stand resolute, but every so often get a direct hit from a big raindrop, and they nod and shudder as it bounces off them. And once I've noticed that with the ivy I can see it happening everywhere else too—sparrow bush, cotoneaster, waxy-leaved bush, blades of grass. Meanwhile the achillea is almost flattened, lying against the holly which is the only thing stopping some of its stems from joining their neighbours flat out on the grass.

Just as the weather is starting to murmur 'autumn', this is the month when the plants too are letting me know the inevitable. The crocosmia are going over, and some of the achillea flowers are starting to fade from burnished yellow to a more pastel shade, although I can see a couple of later cauliflower heads starting to reach up so we'll hopefully have a later burst of them. And the cotoneaster is starting to dull a little—even as it is still growing, the leaves have lost a bit of their lustre. I don't know if that's just because they're not sitting in bright sunlight, or if the bush is finally taking a breather from its efforts of a few months ago when it was producing so many flowers for the bees. It has occasional yellow leaves now, plus a handful of stems which have withered, leaving rust-coloured, dry leaves to punctuate the green.

It's not all withering and drooping here though. The rose is having a second wave of flowering, the lavender is more visible behind the sagging achillea, and the hebe is still hanging onto some purple, this time the newest leaves at the end of each leaf cluster, as though it's trying to prolong the colour even beyond the short life of the flowers. The heathers too are flowering gloriously now—magenta pink and lilac-white give a subtle dash of colour by the door, along with the green and yellow of their leaves. Maybe I should try sketching them. Even the clematis has chucked out another random flower bud out of season, along with the myriad new stems—I vaguely remember that happening before a few years ago too. It's nice to think that even when we think things are done for the season there's still life and surprise waiting for their moment. I don't know why I'm surprised by the clematis though—it's as indestructible and persistent as the fat pigeons!

The lawn still looks scrappy, but not so bad that I need to do anything much about it. It's hardly a wildflower meadow just bursting to thrive, mostly it's just random bits of grass from different commercial seeds. But I do like that it'll never look professionally manicured—it'll never make *Hello!* magazine, and is all the better for that! It's certainly enough of a mish-mash that it's worthy of a bit of attention—who knew that a suburban lawn could be so varied and interesting? There are long thick blades in clumps on the hebe side, thinner blades (different variety) nearer the house, clover leaf near the paving slabs, all intermingling to provide a bit of cover for who knows what living underneath me? Under the hebe there's also ivy creeping into the grass. It always seems completely unfussed by being mown. And despite our best gravelly efforts, the grass is still snaking through the gaps in the paving slabs, resisting any effort to pull it up, and not looking any different if I try to mow it.

The achillea is fascinating to gaze at too—as I watch a banded white-tailed bumblebee checking them out, I can see that the centre of the flower is a tiny cluster of five or six paler blobs, with four or five orange/yellow petals surrounding them. They're so delicate and beautiful, just doing their thing with no regard for me or whether anyone (other than the pollinators) see them or not.

An obvious life lesson for all of us—other than those most important to us, being noticed and admired by others is irrelevant to the wider scheme of things. Just do you because you are awesome.

I've noticed some cotoneaster branches across the front of the compost bin. I should probably cut them back so that it gets the maximum sun to heat it up. Inside the bin, especially round the edges of the lid, are lots of pink skinny worms (I have in my head they're called tiger worms), and some other maggoty-looking things—pretty gross, but if they speed up the food rotting down they're very welcome. I do love the composting process, even when it's gross, and because the bin we have takes all food waste it can get pretty smelly in there. I'll never not be inspired though by the thought of unwanted, dead food and plant remnants rotting down to produce beautiful new full-of-life soil. The world is amazing when you get down to the basics and stop unnecessarily complicating it.

The fat pigeons are making their presence felt this month still, even when they're not here—the garden is covered in white and grey feathers, and when I see the birds they do look much scruffier than usual. There are also shiny turds throughout the lawn and paving labs and I expect the pigeons are the culprits there too. I wish we had hedgehogs in the garden, I'd be quite happy for them to crap everywhere and I'd love these turds to be from hedgehogs not pigeons. I did see a squashed hedgehog by the kerb over the road towards the school, which surprised me as I assumed all the gardens round here were too small to provide a big enough corridor for them to thrive. But I know that's wishful thinking—having watched one of the pigeons taking a giant crap off the top of a telegraph pole out the back, I am certain that they are the ones responsible for the proliferation of poo in the garden.

The pigeon psychological warfare continues unabated too! At one point I looked out of the front window and saw one sitting on the smelly shrub, its weight making the branch lean precariously as the pigeon stared unblinking at me through the window. And now I'm writing in the garden, one of them has been jumping up and down the steps, getting really close, walking across the top of the bush near the conifer, staring at me the whole time. It doesn't give a monkey's that I'm here and can see it. It's also doing low—and pretty close—flypasts, to stop me from relaxing! I kind of admire its persistence, even though I wish it would leave the feeders and give the other birds a chance to feed. They always seem to avoid it when the pigeons are around. Of course, why should the pigeons leave the feeders alone, they're all just doing what comes naturally, and I wish I didn't feel so prejudiced against them. As I watch the pigeon saunter across the top of the bush I feel like Nigel bloody Farage patrolling the white cliffs of Dover for signs of unwanted immigrants, and I hate myself for that. I so want to warm to them more, I hate feeling this guilty and Daily Maily in my own garden!

The sparrows are still around and plentiful too. I love that we have so many here, when further south they've declined since my childhood. I remember them as ten a penny in the 1970s, but although this year's bird survey suggests they're starting to recover, numbers are nowhere near what they were back then. Just in this tiny patch though, I love that there are more sparrows now than there were at the start of the year—at least that one brood has definitely thrived. They're all up in the shrubs by the feeder, chattering away—life is going on entirely as normal for them, even as things continue to be surreal for us.

I can see three sparrows converging on the hebe (could these be Sarah, Percy and Bill?), and a robin sits on the bush near the conifer. They're not being noisy, certainly not compared to a few months ago, but I'm glad to be reminded they're still around. And then a gaggle of sparrows—possibly four, possibly six, too fast to count!—flew in formation from my garden towards the main road, landing in Next Door's buddleia. There was supposed to be a flypast by the Red Arrows of all four of the UK capital cities yesterday for the seventy-fifth anniversary of VJ Day, but that was scuppered by the weather. I'll take my modest sparrow flypast instead. The Red Sparrows? It was good to see the youngsters spreading their wings and getting a bit of speed in, a fleeting but giant burst of energy amongst the general stillness.

The sparrows aren't the only ones doing flypasts. A fat pigeon flies low over my head onto the pavement and is now sitting on the hedge completely unbothered by me. And then it flies down onto the smelly shrub and then straight at me while its partner in crime sits on the fence behind the ceanothus watching what's going on. I'm interpreting this as aggression, of course, but it could just as easily be clumsy curiosity. I'm going to have to figure out how to make my peace with them, because they're here to stay and have as much right to be here as any of the other birds. If we're trying to encourage wildlife in the garden, we can't say some creatures are allowed in and others aren't. But honestly, it would be easier to do that if they were slightly less thuggy!

We're still seeing tits around too, although not as often as before. Usually it's the coal tits still using the feeder, but DreamGirl also pointed out a blue tit that was briefly in the hebe before flying first to one neighbour's garden and then the other's. I'm so happy she's starting to notice things too. I thought I briefly spotted a pied wagtail again, but like the last time, it's probably more likely a coal tit.

During a barbecue out the back recently there was a cacophony of cheeping while we were eating, and we saw a whole gang of birds on the very top of the clock tower, which you can just see from the back, in the gap between Next Door's house and the church hall. HD got his telescope out to zoom in and try and identify them, and it turns out they were starlings. I've only seen one in the garden this year, but at one point watching them up there I counted twenty-six of them! I'd love to see more of them venture down to the garden, they're so beautiful. I wonder if they're the ones making some of the unidentified cheeping I've been hearing recently—quite melodic, not a rasping caw like the crows and gulls. I'm happy that there seems to be such a thriving population nearby—I guess they're nesting in the nature studio, but the top of that tower must be a great place to meet up and check what's going on in the neighbourhood. I hope they check our garden—there's even food there!

The flowers on Next Door's buddleia are starting to turn brown, and I realise I've not seen as many butterflies on it compared to the last couple of years. In fact, I've hardly seen any butterflies at all this year, apart from the few tortoiseshells on our hebe a few weeks ago. I hope next year is better for them—I wonder what's happened this year?

We still have some solitary bees exploring the relatively limited pickings, compared to a couple of months ago. Smelly flower, jasmine, honeysuckle, and heathers are pretty much the only source of nectar at the moment, after the glory days of early summer. A wasp (I think—it could perhaps be a hoverfly, but my unsophisticated identification guessing veers towards wasp) is flying dementedly round the edges of the cotoneaster. I presume the pollinators won't be around much longer. There's just a handful of lone creatures flying slowly and distractedly about, including a massive bumblebee that's just shown up behind me to add its drone to the traffic hum. But with all the flowers now going over, I can't imagine they'll be around much longer.

Mid-month, I spot what looks like a dead brown hebe leaf hanging off one of the crocosmia leaves beneath the peanut feeder. It's that exact shape and length of the older, bigger hebe leaves, but walking round to another angle I can see that it's actually a slug, lighter brown on the other side, bulging as it hangs on. I've left it there, hanging on like a leech. It doesn't seem to have been eating the crocosmia, that doesn't look munched at all. I have though noticed what looks like slime trails on the peanut feeder, and I wonder if it fell off that and landed on the crocosmia? I can't believe in this tiny scrap of garden we're inadvertently nurturing ninja slugs alongside the evil pigeon overlords—maybe we'd better not look to getting a bigger garden after all, we might end up with Jurassic Park!

Checking out the same spot later, and I'm now certain that the slug did indeed fall off the feeder onto the crocosmia. It's still there, and I think it may have actually been impaled by the sharp edges of the crocosmia leaves. Most of it is hanging from the one leaf, but it's in the junction where two leaves meet and there's a bit of slug the other side too, so I think it's met its grisly end. Not so ninja now!

Several days later, and the slug is still there, shrivelled and rotting. I wish the fat pigeons would find it and finish it off, they're more than welcome to it!

As well as the ninja slug, I've noticed a few slime trails by the front step, and out the back there were several slimy trails alongside some smashed shells. I'm not sure which bird was the culprit, but I'm glad they got their meal. We're going to do another nematode treatment later as there are lots of slugs out the back (including occasionally coming indoors) and our vegetable leaves are decidedly lacy-looking! I hope this works.

Just when I'm full of 'slugs and snails are gross' energy, I see a small, entirely black snail crawling up the wall by the front door. Black shell, black body, even black antennae. I've never seen anything like it before, and I have to begrudgingly admit it is quite beautiful. The garden continues to surprise me with the variety of life in such a tiny area.

Recently I learnt that what is now our set of houses that share our back court was once a big church, until sometime in the 1960s. The funny little building over the road was their church hall, apparently. That makes me feel better about our back court, which I must admit I thought had once been cemetery land, so at least there are less likely to be bodies under there! I must try to find some photos online. I'm hoping I can leave this book as a legacy for the house, but it would be nice to have some knowledge of what was here before. When we were in the midst of buying the house we found a YouTube video of its student house days, made by the boys who owned the house before us, but that has (probably wisely) disappeared.

Next Door's house has gone on the market, so I'm feeling a little apprehensive and hope we get good new neighbours. That's natural, I know that the previous owners were nervous when we bought this house and hoped that we'd be good neighbours. I hope we have been! Nothing stays the same though, as less than a year watching the garden has already shown me. Time is marching on, but I think for now I'm going to try and slow down, stop and appreciate what I have in the here and now. I'm just looking round at the plants and bushes, some of which I planted, others which were already here, and drinking in the sight of lush, green life. This tiny garden is so full, it's Tardis-like in the extent of life that is going on while we mostly overlook it and can't see beyond its small dimensions. We are lucky indeed to be here, and rich beyond measure.

I learned while looking through 'the squirrel book' (our guide to UK wildlife, which has a squirrel on the cover hence we've always just called it 'the squirrel book') that Next Door's tree isn't a hawthorn, as I'd wondered, but is actually a rowan. That makes me happy, I've discovered something else, it's like I've made another connection. I think one of the reasons I (and many others) have sometimes felt like a fish out of water in the natural world is not having the words for what I'm seeing, for what's in front of me, so that makes it more alien and uninviting. Now I'm getting these few snippets of basic vocabulary, I can then move on to be more expressive in words, but also allow myself to feel more keenly what I'm experiencing, now I can name some of it.

Seagulls cry out overhead. Even though they're always here, it feels a bit strange—we're just back from a long weekend at the seaside, so have been hearing them by the sea where they 'should' be. But why shouldn't they be here, when we've overfished the seas so they need to look further inland for food? At the moment there's renewed news and panic about migrant boats in the English Channel. I hate this country's outrage at people trying to find shelter and food for themselves and their families whilst staying silent as our politicians sell the arms which are forcing them out of their homes and countries in the first place. And as with politics, so with the environment—we can't rail against seagulls when they're just doing what they need to do, finding food sources where they can, whilst we stay silent about our complicity—more than that, our active acquiescence—in trashing their habitat and the wider food chain on which they depend.

DreamGirl goes back to school for the first time since lockdown in March. She's anxious and excited, which I think is how I feel too. Anxious about the mental health effects of all these months without her friends and the routine and stability of school, plus anxious about how she'll cope with processing everything now she's another year on in school, but excited for her to regain some normality, socialisation, and learning with teachers who actually know what they're doing. Plus of course excited that I can hopefully get back to some sort of routine where I can write more without feeling guilty, and take on more work again and contribute more to the household finances.

SEPTEMBER

After a wet August, I hope that we have one of those second mini-summers which Scotland can be so good at. The month isn't starting too promisingly though. Bright but damp, and the wind is definitely back! There was a super rainbow past the school. It was bright, sunny even, but there was that light mizzle that you can hardly feel until you realise you're soaking, and that was enough for the rainbow to put on its show. The strong breeze is causing the higher trees beyond the church hall to sway pretty violently, as well as Next Door's rowan, and our conifer and hebe, although it doesn't feel dangerous. The sound of the wind in the trees is elemental—even here in deepest suburbia—like the sea crashing onto the shore, here's another reminder that nature can't be boxed and packaged, but will go where it will and do what it does. I know when I watch the trees and bushes in the wind from indoors, it feels so weird seeing all that movement divorced from the sound of susurration.

Some of the wispier clouds are rushing across the sky, and even the big ones are noticeably on the move—it must be a pretty fierce wind up there, even as the blue sky makes it look calm and benign at first glance. I'm not sure if the wind is the reason for the traffic noise seeming louder—it just feels like an aural overload of traffic and lawnmower drones. A couple of cheeps from a sparrow in the hebe reassure me that nature's still here, but I'm finding that retreat into calm not so seamless with all this racket going on.

Autumn is definitely here now. There's often a touch of damp in the air, the local trees are starting to turn yellow and brown at the edges, and the colour overall feels more subdued, less saturated. The rowan berries next door though are cheerfully covering the tree and making me think of the winter berries to come. The tree out the back on which the crows often gather is yellowing quickly, and the park trees are on the turn too. The sun is making a weak attempt to burn off the cloud, not totally successfully, but I can feel its warmth and brightness. It's making all the greens in the garden and on the trees round about very vivid and contrasting—a last gasp of vibrancy before succumbing to the cold and damp that's inexorably on the way.

Greens, yellows and browns are predominating right now in the garden, and in the nearby trees. I've read suggestions this might be a 'mast year'—more fruit and berries than usual—and as well as reflecting the good spring and summer conditions, in folklore a mast year is said to herald a harder than usual winter. This year, of all years, the thought of a harder than usual winter feels hard to take. I am curious to see how the garden responds to frost, ice or snow, in this year when I'm paying particular attention to this little ecosystem, but apart from the potential for slug-suppressing, the prospect of extreme cold isn't too appealing after the year we're still living through.

Two or three sparrows have just done an impressive aerial display from the feeder to the bottom of the sparrow hedge. Their accuracy never ceases to amaze me—obviously they have the advantage of size, but even still, how they don't just crash into everything when they're going at that speed in such an enclosed space is so impressive! In contrast to their speed, the conifer occasionally gives a gentle shudder as a couple of sparrows hop about and pluck up the courage to go to the feeder.

This must be the season for flypasts—a couple of tits (not sure what they are—not very blue or yellow, but too colourful to be coal tits) have just flown from the hebe to the rowan, and I notice they start on one trajectory, then in a split second move up or down a foot or more whilst still carrying on in the same direction. I expect they've been doing that all year, but in the absence of any other distractions today, it's the first time I've noticed and registered it. The sparrows often seem to zoom about in squadrons, and even the fat pigeons have a go, though they are more indecisive and often change their mind and U-turn mid-flight. The raw energy of the smaller birds' sophisticated flypasts is definitely not matched by the Zeppelin-esque pigeons, but God love them, they're not wanting to miss out!

The birds aren't the only ones. There's a sense of anticipation as a Spitfire is due to fly over all of Scotland's hospitals in one day, to say thank you to the NHS, and it's due over the hospital down the road at 2pm, so I should get a good view—especially as for a change the sky is a deep, azure blue and there's barely a cloud to be seen. I have mixed feelings about it—as a gesture it's pretty impressive, but the military connotations make me feel uneasy. There's been a lot of summoning of 'the Blitz spirit' and 'the British spirit' (whatever they are), but WW2 and everything to do with it has been very much co-opted by Nigel Farage and his ilk to exclude and demonise, and make out that the plucky Brits are somehow exceptional and the sooner we go back to Empire and ruling the waves the better, and I want no part of it. And I'm not sure how drawing on past military history and talk of war and victory is appropriate to dealing with a global pandemic—firstly because what is needed is global cooperation, not antagonism, and secondly because the UK political response has been so inept and incompetent and utterly self-serving and uncaring, which doesn't sound much like the mythical Blitz spirit to me.

I look up at the blue sky and wispy cloud and listen to a bit of cheeping and chirping amongst the traffic hum, and it all feels so very incongruous, and like this little corner of reality is so very unreal.

I have to admit though, the Spitfire was very impressive, especially the sound it made, which I heard before I saw it. The next day I watch two sparrows do a low flypast, every bit as impressive as the Spitfire, even though their audience of one is considerably less impressive!

They're not always entirely accurate though. One poor sparrow just flew from the conifer straight into the front window and back again. Luckily it wasn't a hard contact and it didn't knock itself out. I'm not sure what it thought it was doing—the blind was down so it was very clear that it was a hard surface and not a clear space.

I'm wearing my new glasses, so my vision feels a bit distorted till I get used to them. There's probably some sort of metaphor in there somewhere, but the birds are cheeping and peeping quite loudly (coal tits mainly, I think), and I'd sooner listen to them than dredge up a tortured analogy from the depths of my limited imagination! I've just refilled the seed feeder, worms and water, and it looks like something's had a go at the fatball, plus the peanuts are continuing to go down, so the best-fed birds in Stirling are still doing OK for themselves!

The tits are skitting about from hebe to feeder and cotoneaster, it's lovely to see them having their turn—it's usually the sparrows that I can see. Plus the fat pigeons, of course. Currently all I can see of them is even more shed feathers and splats of gooey turds.

A change in the usual background noise is a seagull and couple of jackdaws fighting over a discarded bread roll in the middle of the street—at least it makes a change from the constant traffic and lawnmower noise. There aren't so many of the usual bird calls—I guess as we head into autumn and winter they're preserving their energy more, and I must admit to looking forward to seeing the differences in how they interact with the garden. I've not seen the blackbirds or robin for a while, but I do remember them both being around last winter (and both featuring in our Big Garden Birdwatch tally), so I hope they remember us and start visiting again.

The bird calls haven't stopped completely though. The tits call musically, the sparrows still cheep, and I also catch a more melodic call but can't see who is doing the singing. I'm going to guess robin or blackbird, still not showing themselves but hopefully not far away. I'm trying to imagine the traffic hum as a musical drone, but it's a struggle. It was much easier to make the imaginative leap with the humming of the bees and flies in summer. Sadly they're pretty much silent now, hopefully hunkering down and doing what they've got to do to ensure the next generation can do their thing next year.

There's a big flock of black birds flying overhead. They sound more melodic than crows, but I don't think they're blackbirds. Maybe it's the gang of starlings we saw on the clock tower the other week? What I'd love is to see a full-on murmuration, but there's not enough of them for that here. Life dreams!

The sparrows descend onto the conifer and from there down to the seeds, and displace what I think might have been a long-tailed tit—infrequent but always welcome visitors here. It had grabbed a bit of fatball and then a beakful of seeds, and retired to a branch on the smelly bush to eat its prize. A coal tit has now arrived, and looking at its tail I'm more sure the previous bird was indeed a long-tailed tit. It's a bit frustrating that sometimes they're so fast that identification has to be by process of elimination, but I'm happy either way that the long-tailed tit was here! And now the sparrows and tits are zooming between the feeder, conifer, and Next Door's rowan. The rowan is such a beauty, I hope the new owner appreciates it. The red berries are so bright against the deep blue sky, it makes me think of a quirky fabric pattern, the colours are so cheerful. I'd definitely wear a dress made of that!

A tit which I am struggling to identify—possibly a coal tit, but it looks a bit yellowy on the front so I wonder if it's a juvenile blue tit—is busy flitting from feeder to cotoneaster to feeder to sparrow hedge. Whatever it is, it's making a right mess of the seeds, which are flying about all over the place. It is a beauty though, even though its table manners leave a bit to be desired! Now it adds the ceanothus, hebe and garden wall to its flitting route, and is already back at the feeder—it's such a joy to watch it patrolling and eating its fill.

And the lovely robin has returned, for the first time in ages—I bet that was the singer of the melodic song I heard the other day. It's sat regally on the cordyline stump, checking out what's new. I hope it's back for good.

The feeders are filled up again—it feels like the seed feeder is emptied in a single day at the moment, just like in early spring. I guess the birds are stocking up while they can, ready for winter. I've seen both tits and sparrows, plus of course the fat pigeon, which was sitting in the tray earlier hoovering up the spilled seeds. We saw a squirrel earlier in the hebe trying to get at the peanuts (not very successfully), and there have been plenty of birds having a go at the peanuts too, so I'm glad that's meeting a need.

To end the month, a glorious sight as I got home from the school run—I was at the front door shuffling about with my keys, and a flock of noisy starlings landed in Next Door's rowan tree. They were squabbling and going for the berries. I suspect they're not going to last very long! Then they'd mostly fly off, and return almost immediately for more, like a suburban mini-murmuration. The weather is foul wet, but seeing that gave me such a lift!

The peanut feeder is covered in slug slime, so I think once it's been emptied by the birds I might put some copper tape on it and see if that makes any difference. It helped our potted plants previously, although I am still amused by the slug I caught one time trying to shimmy over the tape, one end still planted below the tape while it tried to reach the top of the pot without touching the copper.

I've noticed a couple of the teeny tiny baby snails on the front door in the last couple of days. Last year we had loads, hopefully the smaller number this year is a good sign for fewer snails next year. But even though they're pests, they're so delicate and perfectly formed, just a little dot a millimetre or two across, that I'm filled with wonder. Nature is so amazing.

I've caught another ninja slug in the act—it was on the outside of the tray hanging beneath the peanut feeder, going for the birds' leftovers. It wasn't there later, and hadn't been impaled by the crocosmia leaves, so presumably lived to see (and eat) another day. As well as the feeder, there are quite a few slug trails on the paving slabs, and I saw a big black one there yesterday. I didn't tread on it, I couldn't bear the splat, and I hoped one of the birds might get it. Why do the slugs ignore the food/compost bin? When I had a compost bin in my garden in London it was always full of slugs. To give them their due, they did a great job of speeding up the decomposition and made beautiful compost. Here though they're nowhere to be found in the compost. The tiger worms, and whatever the maggoty eggs are, are there, but not a slug in sight despite it looking like slug heaven. Maybe it's the coffee grounds in there. Perhaps I should start keeping those separate and put them under the ivy below the hebe, see if that puts them off there and encourages them towards the compost instead?

Later on, out of the corner of my eye I see the still upstanding leaves of the killer crocosmia waving frantically in the breeze. I am enjoying the view, then guess what I spot? Another ninja slug, impaled in exactly the same place as the last one! Maybe this will be my lasting contribution to natural slug control: plant crocosmias beneath your bird feeders! It's completely coincidental, but it is perfectly placed guilt-free anti-slug measures. This slug is smaller than the last one, but just as dead—good (natural) riddance!

I've also spotted a couple of bigger slugs, with spotty heads and stripy bodies, black and brown, on the peanut feeder and on the front step. I'm not keen to Google it. Who wants to look at a page of slug pictures? It might though be worth checking if they're the type of slug which eats other slugs, in which case I can be a bit more forgiving of them!

Looking up, a brief movement catches my eye. At the base of the gutter, as it meets the drainpipe, a spider's web is shimmering in the breeze and catching the sunlight. Earlier, as I left for work, it was misty and a web in the front gate greeted me, silver threads stretched out to catch the moisture and whatever else fell under its spell. Those webs are so beautiful. I just wish they didn't herald the indoors-march of the spiders, who despite my best efforts to like them do make me shudder when they scuttle about inside!

The achillea flowers are stubbornly hanging on—still yellow, although starting, maybe, to brown and dry a little. Still beautiful though, and welcome colour, although I wonder if I should put in a stake or two to stop them leaning over quite so much? I can also see some rust-covered leaves on a lower branch of the evergreen conifer by the feeder, but the rust colour seems almost vibrant, particularly in contrast to the mostly brown of the smelly flowers next to it. Maybe it's just vibrant-looking in this light, and would be duller when it's grey and raining?

Below the hebe, on the lawn, older yellow leaves lie after being shed, along with dry and shrivelling brown ones. I'm not sure the lawn needs any mulching, but I imagine the hebe offering the leaves to nourish the ground underneath, and I feel gratitude for the gift. Much like a child, what they can give isn't much in the eyes of the world, but is so precious, and should be received with grace.

More colour with a handful of leaves at the side of the cotoneaster a bright coppery orange/yellow, in contrast to the bulk which remain a resolutely dark green. I do love that burnt orange colour—even as the season is cooling and turning, it is such a warm tone that makes me think of hunkering down in front of an open fire.

The grass is looking scruffy again, but it's too wet to mow. The greens throughout the garden are bright after their drenching, even while the yellow of the achillea is fading fast, and the smelly flowers are dropping the very last of their white petals. Who knew you could have this many greens in one tiny space?

The achillea is still leaning on the holly, but this has given the lavender a bit more of a look-in at the sunlight and there are still a handful of dark purple flowers. The other side of the garden, the silver sands I planted out doesn't look so well, it's pretty brown and doesn't look very alive. Behind it though the crocosmia leaves are catching the sunlight and the vertical stripes of their veins along the length of the tall leaves are distinctive and add yet another pattern to the garden palate.

The purply-pinks and whites of the heather are still proclaiming their beauty. This is their time to shine, while the sedum is now red and homely-looking. It reminds me of the red of ripening blackberries, before they turn black and ready to pick. Which reminds me of all the foraged fruit (blackberries and elderberries) I still have in the freezer from last year—I think it may be crumble time soon!

The waxy-leaved shrub has new berries, still green, as well as a couple of red ones which I think have hung on all year since last winter. The deep, dark green of the leaves seems so solid—full of life and sap, which is presumably why some of them have been nibbled by something. The holly is that same dark green, and is still propping up the top-heavy achillea. Even though they're both evergreen, there's something about the darkness and smoothness of their leaves which anticipates winter, waiting to come into their own.

Beyond the garden, the trees in the park and behind the church hall are definitely turning yellow. I'm reminded of a passage in Emma Mitchell's *The Wild Remedy* which helped me look at the falling and changing colours of the leaves differently—the yellows and oranges are always there, but in spring and summer it's the green of the chlorophyll that is dominant. In autumn the trees are taking the chlorophyll back into themselves for winter, which is why we can see the yellows and browns for a season. It's a reminder to me of how death and life are always intertwined, it's not a case of one or the other, but they are both held together in tension and each sustains the other through the yearly cycle.

The acorn we planted a couple of years ago, still on the front windowsill, is now about four inches high, with four leaves—a brilliant reminder that oaks work on entirely different time frames to us. When we first planted it, we put it, along with three others we'd picked up, in vermiculite and covered it for a while, but this is the only one of the four which not only sprouted but also didn't go mouldy. Each and every leaf has been an excitement. The biggest leaf is on its own, just over halfway up the stem, with a cluster of old leaf joints where most of the original baby leaves were. Then about an inch and a half further up, three more leaves fan out like helicopter blades, with what might be—I hope—the start of a further bit of stem about to grow even higher. I've no idea what will happen to this oak. I feel a huge sense of responsibility that, having got it this far, we must give it its best shot. I know being on a windowsill in a centrally-heated house won't be the best thing for ever, and I want to do the best for this little plant, germinating and growing where the others didn't. I'm also utterly mindblown by the thought that this tiny stem, only a couple of millimetres in diameter, could in decades and centuries to come be a huge solid trunk harbouring hundreds of different creatures and life forms. Wow, I think I've achieved so much, but this little tree has a potential legacy that far, far outstrips mine. I'm in the presence of true greatness.

I'm aware of some shoots of ivy that I missed in the last pruning, reaching up to the hebe's lower branches, and also snaking across the ground, covering the bases of the crocosmias and reaching even as far as the cordyline. I do like the cover it provides, and who knows how many invertebrate species, and even birds, it is sheltering, but it feels like I need to be constantly on the watch to make sure it doesn't smother everything in its path. I don't want it to be super tidy, all neat borders, and I like how it blurs so many boundaries in the garden. But I also don't want to have a sea of ivy covering the garden at the expense of everything else. So I've stopped feeling guilty about cutting it back—it's a brilliant habitat, but my gentle pruning doesn't seem to stop it at all, and within a few weeks it is always as vigorous as ever with no obvious detriment, and the nearby plants are given a bit more of a chance to not be completely swamped.

Even now we're heading well and truly into autumn, there are still plenty of buds around. The largest of the three new rose stems is already sporting a couple of buds, so even though the older leaves aren't looking great, the rose is clearly not giving up just yet! The random clematis bud I spotted the other week is now fully open, defying the season. I know it won't last long, but the clematis' last gasp for the year (along with the new shoots it's still throwing out) brings me such joy—yet another reminder of life going on despite 'the rules.'

In the nature studio, the hawthorn berries are out in extravagant abundance. Unfortunately so are the midges, so we can never stay for long, but those berries are glorious! I don't know if they're like that every year, but certainly this year there are rich pickings for any bird who wants them!

A pigeon feather and various leaves, plus some seeds which look like dandelion seeds except it's the wrong time of year for dandelions, whizz past my seat on the lawn, while the more rooted and weighed down elements of the garden rock and bend and shake in the wind. I'm finding it quite exhilarating—despite being something of a middle-class, suburban enclave, it's yet another reminder that I don't need Attenborough levels of wildlife to feel connected to the land and to this place.

Society feels in such a weird limbo right now. People are largely complying with masks in shops, school seems a haven of normality even though they're obviously changing some routines, and it doesn't feel like there's that sense of impending danger and heightened stress like there was in March. But, there's still no covid vaccine, the conspiracy theorists are out in force, and infection rates are going up again. We're not seeing as many deaths as at the start of it all, but I fear for the longer-term consequences: the long-term aftereffects for people who were infected, and the rush back to an economically greedy and unequal 'solution' to the issues of unemployment and job uncertainty, rather than taking the chance to look at a new way of living. And that's before we even think about the impact of Brexit and the upcoming US election (which I am scared Trump will win). The world we live in isn't tranquil, despite the tranquillity in the garden and the lessons I can learn about slowing down, being thankful for the small things, and letting go of pointless materialistic ambition. I still don't know for sure how to live authentically in it and make a positive difference.

At the pool today, one of my fellow swimmers, an older gentleman, asked us if we thought all this social distancing was making us more antisocial as a society. Pretty sure he was angling for a 'yes.' I said I thought we were 'differently social' now (which earnt me A Look), but I'm glad I was able to make the point that I think we've—on the whole—become more thoughtful about other people's space. Which got me thinking about the garden, and this writing project—I love sharing the space with DreamGirl, but only as long as I'm not writing or working. I struggle with the interruptions to my concentration, and then feel guilty, like I'm blaming or trying to exclude her. I'm not trying to do that, of course, I love it when we're both out here and she notices new (or rather, previously unnoticed) things. But now that I'm more emotionally invested in this project, I need to work out what's an appropriate boundary for my work and what is just being exclusionary. It's hard to be radically inclusive in such a small garden, but the flowers and shrubs and bees and birds and slugs manage to get by fine side-by-side in the same space. I know they're physically smaller than me, but I'd love to work out a genuine attitude shift that would make me more open and welcoming here. I need to remember that, among the seasonal flux, the evolution and growing and dying off and renewal, is also a place to slow down and relax that is constant. And that can't just be for me.

A lovely break from covid reality came when my aunt and uncle popped round on their way home from their Highland holiday, and we spent a couple of hours catching up over a pub meal. I realised when they'd gone that they're the first family we've seen face to face, not over Zoom or Skype, for this entire year. My heart is aching, even as I was so happy to see them—this year has cost all of us so much.

I was reading a collection by renowned Scottish poet, Norman MacCaig, and it sparked further reflection on what I'm learning here in the garden this year. Of course now I can't find the first poem that I want, but it was talking about garden birds and plants not knowing what they are—the sparrow has no conception of being called a sparrow, a rose doesn't know it's a rose, they just ARE, and live as themselves. And I was thinking about my preoccupation with wanting to know what different birds and insects and plants are, and I think it's because with that knowledge, ostensibly of a wider vocabulary, I have more of a sense of belonging. Yet these creatures and plants, who surely 'belong' more naturally and intuitively than I ever will, have no perception of such things as language and vocabulary in the same way. That's not to say their 'communication' is meaningless, I think my observations this year prove that that isn't the case. But they don't need to 'name' or possess in order to belong. Which then got me thinking about MacCaig's poem *A Man in Assynt*—it talks about ownership, and possession of land, asking who possesses the land: the millionaire who buys it, or I who am possessed by it? From there it's also got me thinking about the Creation myth and the Garden of Eden—I always think that Adam and God naming things must have been such fun, but does it distance us from these beautiful creatures if we give them names that they themselves have no clue about? Ultimately there's no answer for any of these questions, but I do love how feeling closer to a particular space in the world is making me more open to questions in literature and religion.

This month marks the fifteenth anniversary of me moving to Scotland. I've now been here nearly as long as I lived in London, which I can't believe, given that London felt like home for so long. By this point in London I was ready to move on and had had enough of big city life, whereas here I still feel totally and utterly at home—it's been a good move for me, I'm very thankful to live in such a beautiful spot in such a beautiful country.

OCTOBER

The rain is falling softly, almost silently apart from the occasional patter on the umbrella. I can see it falling, and catching the breeze, sometimes vertical, sometimes at a slight angle, this way or that. But although I see it falling, I can't see it landing. The leaves are still, and have older droplets on them, but I can't see any water disturbance on them. The gentle misty rain caresses the ground it is nourishing and soaking. The still droplets pick out individual blades of grass and clover leaves, and reflect back the white of the overcast sky, a starscape gazing up at me, unblinking. The hebe flowers and smelly flowers, brown and bowed after their vibrant brief summer blooming, look solemn and pensive, but not defeated.

The first of the season's named storms, Storm Alex, is on its way. The evening before is calm and sunny, so I take the Vitamin D fix while I still can. The clock tower glows golden in the sunlight against the pale blue sky, and I notice the leaves on the sparrow bush are yellower too.

In Alex's aftermath, everything is newly-washed—fresh, not bedraggled. In fact, apart from the achillea, the garden feels like it has quite perked up after its soaking. Heavy grey clouds quickly blow over to leave blue sky and white cloud. I should look at the clouds more often—DreamGirl points out a wispy one she thinks looks like a dinosaur footprint (I can't see it myself), but it soon goes, replaced with bigger cloud, still white but more solid looking. I guess the winds must be strong up there, the cloud shapes are shifting so quickly and moving on, although I can hardly feel a breeze down here. I'm enjoying the slight pressure of the sun on my face while I still can.

Much of the rest of the month is relentlessly wet. Between showers I sit out in the wind—the tree beyond the church hall is being buffeted and thrown about, like waves crashing against the shore. Less wave-like, but equally buffeted, is Next Door's plastic shed, the roll-up walls and doors straining at every seam, offering little protection to the plants and shed skeleton within. I remember we had a similar shed a few years ago that took such a battering in one storm (it might even have been the legendary Storm Bawbag) that the poles and plastic cover were all over the back court, and we ended up having to bin it as some of the poles were so bent. I guess the wind was just giving us a wee reminder that just because we can't see it doesn't mean it's not there and out to cause chaos.

The wind and heavy rain suit my mood, as I heard that I'm likely to be redeployed back to the ward again because of covid and winter pressures on the health service. So, despite both neighbours and husband thinking I'm nuts, I need to sit out here regardless of the weather, and breathe in fresh air and watch the life that is available to me today at its most elemental.

The sky is a monochrome grey, and completely opaque—there's no indication that there's any distance or horizon, it just stops above the trees. The relentless patter of the rain on the umbrella is complemented with regular drips from the drainage pipes, and the individual drips jumping from leaf to leaf till they hit the ground with a splat. The splatting is especially loud when the raindrop falls from the hebe onto the carpet of ivy leaves on the ground, which give an exaggerated shudder and shake, like a dog that's just emerged from a swim.

The hebe branches are weighed down with the non-stop water; it slides effortlessly off the newer leaves, before getting trapped in the dead brown flowers. The carpet of yellow hebe leaves on the lawn look limp and forlorn, as they brown off and slowly return to the soil.

Beneath the conifer, behind the newly refilled feeder, the little den looks fresh and vibrant. The cordyline and errant hebe shoots are bright and cheerful, drinking up the water while sheltered from the full brunt of it. Looking back at the hebe, and the ivy behind it, they strike me as much more stoic and resigned, gritting their teeth and putting up with the conditions.

I know the feeling.

The waxy-leaved shrub has some berries turning orange, before the full-on red of winter. It'll be good to have some dots of red when most of the garden colour is much more subdued for a season. There seems to be quite a bit more browning among the conifer leaves—there are rusty browns and a bit of yellow among the dark greens—and I wonder if it's a bad sign? Most of the brown is on the lower branches, but I can also see some near the top of the tree too.

A tiny magenta flower on the most pruned of the heathers, below the honeysuckle and rose, suddenly sings its presence, and I'm glad that maybe my pruning wasn't a complete disaster after all. It does still look a bit heavily-shorn, all these months later, so I'm grateful for any signs of life. Across the steps, the other more vigorous heather flowers are starting to fade. I can still see the pink, but it's an elderly pink rather than being in the first flush of youth (can relate).

The pyracantha, normally quite swamped by ivy and squashed against the front wall, has a handful of orange-red berries too. I'm glad it didn't get completely buried under the ivy—I know pyracantha is a very suburban plant, but I do like those white dot flower buds in the summer and the colour from the berries (and hopefully more food for the birds) later on. One of the lower rose buds is also close to opening, while the higher up flowers are still displaying themselves beautifully among the general green-yellow-brownness of the garden.

Next door's rowan tree's leaves are turning coppery-brown now, so it's harder to make out what's left of the berries now they no longer have a green backdrop. We'll be able to see the streetlamp beyond the tree soon, once the leaves fall. I want them to hang on as long as possible, but life goes on, so bare branches, beautiful in their own way, will be the norm soon enough. The blackbird is back, bouncing on a thin branch as it chases the remaining berries. As well as resolving to have a ceanothus, giant hebe and cotoneaster in the garden if we ever move, I'm now hankering for a rowan as well, now that I've seen how bountiful and beautiful it is throughout the year.

The sparrow hedge and toilet brush hedge (which hasn't flowered at all this year—quite right, 2020 doesn't deserve its exuberance) will be dropping their leaves too, so I'll be able to see a bit more of the sparrows' and tits' acrobatics soon.

The first of the lower cluster of rosebuds has opened out, while the upper bunch are still going strong, they've lasted much longer than usual. I guess they must be well-sheltered by the honeysuckle they're peering through. There are blobs of red all over—the roses the most prominent, of course, but as I work my way round the garden there's also small blocks of red leaves on the cotoneaster, and red berries on the waxy-leaved bush and pyracantha. All the other flowers that are still out—achillea, heather—are fading fast, so I'm glad for the red to stop it from being too drab too soon. Not that I begrudge a bit of autumn drabness—the garden was pulsating with energy throughout spring and summer, so I can forgive it for wanting to chill out a bit and be less showy.

There are more hebe leaves on the lawn now, and despite the rain, quite a bit of the grass, especially the longer and thicker blades of grass are browning too. The sparrows are calling, but apart from them and the welcome reds throughout the garden, everything else is subdued, dull, letting the last of their energy go before the arrival of the cold winter months.

Looking up, the hebe, ceanothus and conifer show a green silhouette against the grey-white of the clouds above. The remains of the summer's hebe flowers are at their best here—they might be on their last gasp, but I can see every individual blob and hair of each flower, and it reminds me again of the Biblical verses about God knowing every hair of my head, every sparrow that falls. They might not be Solomon in all his splendour, but I find the quiet dignity of these nearly-dead blooms surprisingly moving—an unexpected reminder to remember my own significance.

The hebe continues to yellow and shed yet more leaves. Next Door's (towards the main road) hedge is also yellow, but somehow it's a more vibrant and energetic yellow. They'll all go the same way eventually, of course, but it's interesting how one speaks to me of quiet resignation, and the other is more defiant. Meanwhile, the ivy, which I only cut back a couple of weeks ago, is already putting out young-green new shoots—it's a non-stop job, trying to stop it from taking over the hebe completely! The older ground level ivy is also on the march, it's reached the cordylines the other side of the garden, and I'll probably have to give that a prune as well at some point.

The lower rose has collected some rain and is valiantly hanging on to it, cupping its petals round the precious giver of life. The upper roses are starting to look a bit tatty round the edges, even in their shelter, so the next lot of big wind will probably see some rose petal confetti over the lawn. There's more colour elsewhere with the cotoneaster diversifying even more—when I first noticed yellow and red leaves it was individual branches, but now the yellow leaves especially are dotted about a bit more, giving it a bit of a yellow-green 'salt and pepper' look. As someone who's rocking the salt and pepper myself (particularly the salt, if I'm honest!) I do approve!

In the space of just a couple of days, Next Door's rowan has shed most of its leaves—there's a handful of full fronds still, but they're vastly outnumbered by partial fronds and rapidly emptying branches. The tree beyond the church hall is still full of leaves, but they're turning a subdued brown, and will be bare before too long. Looking the other way, towards the park, the trees I can see are definitely thinning on top too, and I'm going to have to face the inevitable.

Nearby, the autumn colours of the trees in the nature studio have been absolutely glorious. I drove past when the sky was that amazing blue that Scotland does so well, and the oranges in particular seemed to be singing lustily, like *Last Night of the Proms* but less cringey, before their long winter sleep.

At the end of the month I spotted something I've not seen in the garden before—enormous mushrooms growing at the foot of the honeysuckle. They're a pale beige and would be big as saucers if there was enough room for them to spread out. There's none where HD sowed the mushroom spawn earlier in the year, so I don't trust this to eat, and will leave them for the creatures who know what they are! I don't know where they've come from—turns out small town mysteries aren't just for the cosy crime books!

The peanut feeder is covered in slime again, just at the top. I've started separating out the coffee grounds from the rest of the food waste, and will see if a generous spreading of coffee underneath the ivy by the feeder makes any difference. A more immediate concern though is the cloud of midges I can see caught by the sunlight—they look like the Glow Buzzers from *The Clangers*, but much less benevolent!

It's not taken long to find out who's sliming the top of the feeder. I've just spotted the most HUMUNGOUS slug sitting on the lid, lounging around like Jabba the Hutt (and nearly as big!), like it owned the place. I tried to dislodge it with my umbrella, but it was having none of it. I must try and find the copper tape—a certain amount of sluggage I can put up with, albeit begrudgingly, but there is no way that this garden is big enough for a giant like that one!

At the base of the seed feeder, my eye catches a tiny flash of movement. A creepy-crawly, possibly a worm, or maybe centipede (although it looks too smooth and thin to be a centipede), covered in some of the smaller seeds, seems to be dragging them along. At first I think it's burying them, but I think that was an optical illusion, and in fact it was just lengthening and contracting its body in propulsion. I turn my head, distracted by a coal tit, and when I turn back it's gone, presumably either underground or in the longer grass, but I'm happy for a sign we're helping to nourish the invertebrates we can barely see, as well as the more obvious birds above ground.

Other than the odd slime trail on the paving slabs, I think the coffee ground mulch just might be doing the trick, as I've not seen a single actual slug since. Now we just need them to find the compost bin and we (and they) are sorted.

A movement catches my eye—there's a robin in the depths of the corner den below the conifer, hopping from the lower trunks of the smelly and waxy-leaved bushes. I'm so glad it's becoming a regular again, I hope I hear it call soon. Not that I can hear anything right now as a council worker has just turned on either a strimmer or hedge cutter—in this rain!—so I shall have to enjoy the robin's exploration of the nether regions of the den and the innards of the cotoneaster with an annoying soundtrack. I can hear a bit of cheeping—tits, I think—but then I get the mechanical drone in stereo, as towards the main road another council worker has started cutting the grass. The noise is relentless. Once again, as so often this year, I crave not silence but definitely no engine noise! Argh, will you just shut up!

The activity every time I sit out here is still frenzied. A coal tit appears from nowhere, takes a couple of seeds and flies off again. On the paving slabs near the gate, the familiar heavy wing beats of not one but two fat pigeons—I'm not sure if they're squaring up to each other or what's going on, but there's a lot of flapping and invading of each others' space, although it's over almost as soon as it's begun. And then a group of three coal tits fly at the feeder at some speed. One grabs some seed in a quick flypast, and they're off again. I wonder if they can sense the impending change of weather?

One of the coal tits is coming back again and again, not remotely bothered by me sitting here in a bright red fleece—I'm not even camouflaged! I bet I'd see so much more if we had the room for a proper hide. A couple of sparrows zoom out of the hedge like bullets, and the coal tit comes back first for a drink and then to eat (and chuck more seeds on the ground). I'm struck again how hard I find it to recognise the bird calls, single cheeps and chirps. Some of the sounds I think might be the handful of starlings on the clock tower, and in the other direction I think there may be more tits, but I can't be sure without seeing them. Then a new call—'p-tsooooo'—with a slightly descending note, less than a semitone, and I'm frustrated again that I can't identify what's around me.

The robin picks this moment to land on the smelly bush, accompanied by a 'chip-chip-chip-p'peep' which might be the robin but I can't be completely sure. Just like when I'm abroad and feel like I'm missing out on much of what's going on, because I can't fully follow what I'm hearing, this feels similar. There's a sudden burst of a more melodic call, and I wish that I could be let in a little bit more to this amazing world. The robin and coal tit seem to be playing tag, from the feeder to the hebe to Next Door's rowan. The robin is currently calling 'tseep'—I managed to see its beak open and hear the sound coming out, so I know I'm attributing that one correctly!

And now the sparrows are here too, three or four of them. I love watching this non-stop activity, after a couple of much more subdued bird months. I hope they still come in winter, and know they will be fed and cared for. Certainly I feel like I'm mainly focusing on the birds when I'm out here, but that is because they're the main activity I can see going on at the moment. It's great to see how active they are, as they start to build up for winter. The feeder is being almost emptied every day, with loads of seeds on the ground. The pigeons and robin have been hoovering up a lot of the seeds on the ground, and there'll be plenty for them as the tits seem so manic and urgent right now as they put their heads in the feeder and shower seeds left and right and all over the place!

Right now I can see a coal tit chucking out as many seeds as it's eating, extravagantly tossing out the seeds that are not to its taste! I think a lesson about extravagance and only settling for the best might be a good, if somewhat incongruous, lesson to learn in these weird and straitened times. HD says he's seen the blackbirds back too, so at least there's another bunch of birds to feast on the coal tit's leftovers!

The legalities are going to be finalised soon for the house sale next door, and I'm really hoping our new neighbour keeps the rowan tree in his front garden. I thought I saw a blackbird in the rowan as I walked past yesterday, but then a whole flock flew out of the tree and up to the clock tower, so I'm pretty sure it was starlings not blackbirds this time.

The starlings are flying over the house now—there was another flock (or maybe it was the same one) flying over a few minutes ago. The sky is where the action is at today! I thought they might land on the clock tower, but they are quite a bit higher up than that. Earlier I spotted a starling for a split second in the garden—it landed on the hebe, big red rowan berry in its beak, but flew off again as quickly as it arrived. Around the same time I also saw a flash of a magpie, but like the starling it was a blink and you'll miss it visit. And the flock of starlings have flown over again, gossiping as they fly—I bet it's actually the same group doing several circuits overhead. Having been quite slobby recently I feel jealous of their speed and freedom—I'll have to get out for the rest of the week and use up a bit of energy. And here come the starlings again—like the Spitfire last month, I hear them before they come into view.

The rowan is quite a site for bird action this month. I've been watching a male blackbird happily going at the berries, and now he's been joined by a gaggle of starlings. They've all gone after a bit of argy-bargying, but they'll be back soon. Most of the starlings are now on the clock tower—I bet they've got a brilliant view from there, and I'll look as small to them at that distance as they do to me.

There's also something hopping about in the hebe, I think a great tit, and a coal tit just did a ninja fly-in, chucked some seeds about and flew off again. I'm glad to see the peanut feeder is being used too—I copper-taped the top and round the top of the tray, so it looks like a cheap shiny prop from *Blake's 7* and I worried that it would put off the birds as well as the slugs. So far so good though—birds are still visiting, and I've not seen any slugs, so I'm pleased with that!

DreamGirl still comes out here with me sometimes, and on this occasion she's decided she's going to commune with the birds. Over her whistling attempts at bird calls I can hear starlings chattering and sparrows calling, and just for a minute the unceasing traffic hum is at least relegated to an ostinato drone below the real music of birds and child.

I've started seeing a bit more of the sparrows too; it's felt like they've kept a lower profile recently , but they're back at the feeder, sharing it with the tits. The sparrows are much tidier feeders in comparison—head in, eat, finish, fly off, job done—unlike the tits, who are currently beak in, chuck it all about, trying to get that one particular seed they want further in. The sparrows do have to work quite hard though to get a chance at the feeder—this really does seem to be the season where the coal tits especially are trying to consume as much as possible and sod the mess, so there's definitely not much genteel British queueing going on!

The news is its usual dire self, of course. Trump has covid, the US election is only a month away, the UK government is spectacularly botching both Brexit and covid, and in Scotland it looks like we'll have to go into a 'circuit breaker' lockdown. Because of that we're probably going to have to cancel our holiday in Skye, which is hard—we all could so do with a break! But life is buzzing on in the garden—there's a cacophony of bird calls and zooming and feeding, as it should be.

I'm feeling anxious again. Nicola Sturgeon has already said it's not going to be a full lockdown, and while part of me is relieved it's not going to be like March again, I'm also feeling anxious about the less than full measures—just shut us down completely for a couple of weeks and bring the number of cases down! I'm being selfish, of course—our jobs are safe (for now), we're not working in hospitality which is likely to be hardest hit, and it's the two-week school holiday anyway so we don't have to worry about keeping DreamGirl off school. But we knew where we were with full lockdown (even though where we were was horrible), whereas now with more leeway people are relaxing and taking more risks. Whatever happens, at least I have this space to retreat and recentre myself, but I am craving a mythical normality at the moment.

In the midst of wanting certainty and stressing out about the lack of it in the midst of the pandemic, though, insignificant things that I don't have to do anything about other than appreciate in the moment are very appealing. Though that could also be my lack of energy talking, as I'm tired and trying to fight off an infection. Out here in the garden I find I'm appreciating both the solid, cyclical-but-basically-the-same-every-year-ness of it all, but also the more ephemeral, blink-and-you'll-miss it aspects, like cloud formations and fleeting bird visits. I just want to sit, look, and appreciate. Not even notice, particularly, just live in the moment and then be done with it. Must be too tired to be profound! Ultimately though, if I'm going to do what needs doing to just get through the day, then this is a lovely spot for it, and I'm grateful yet again.

There's a van idling in the street which is winding me up—what is the point of that? DreamGirl gave the van driver a fierce look that I'd never have got away with (oh to be six again!), and he at last has reversed around the corner and gone away. I need to cultivate the 'disapproving child' look, maybe I could get rid of more unwanted background hum. Mind you, my looks and stares aren't making any difference to the pigeons, so I think I still need to work on it! DreamGirl has just said how annoying she's finding the traffic noise, and I'm pleased that she's noticed even while I'm also sad. We did though have a pleasant little reverie imagining ourselves living somewhere rural where we don't have to strain our ears to hear the birds over the traffic drone.

It's the end of the month, raining, and most of my awareness is taken up by the sound of the rain being blown onto the umbrella, individual drips from plant to ground, and traffic hum, with my visual field shrunken by the umbrella obscuring the sky. I usually get to enjoy this sort of weather without being disturbed, as everyone else is far too sensible to sit out getting soaked, but today I was caught in the act by a delivery driver.

'Enjoying the sun?' he quipped.

I replied that this was my calm place and I was here for my mental health.

He nodded and seemed to get it, although I still think that he's another one to add to my 'thinks I'm a bit dotty' list, which I must admit is getting quite long now!

Despite the diminished view and crappy weather, I feel the need to breathe in this little patch of green more than ever, especially if the ward redeployment goes ahead. Over the year it has become so important for me to recalibrate in green space when I'm stressed. It almost doesn't matter which green space. I could sit under a tree in the nature studio or at the park. But being in the space I know makes me feel more 'held,' connected to something bigger than me and my insignificant circumstances.

NOVEMBER

Sometimes I just have to write from the comfort of the living room. In the aftermath of Storm Aidan, it's raining and forecast to get worse. It's strange not hearing the wind and rain and bird calls, but I'm not missing the traffic hum! Of course, now I'm indoors the sun is trying to peek out—I'm not going to disturb the sparrows clustering round the feeder, though. Their needs are more important than mine right now.

Aidan's winds have blown the old hebe leaves all over the lawn, plus quite a lot of the dead brown flowers. The wind was pretty impressive. From indoors I could hear the bins clattering about, but seeing the dead flowers strewn over the lawn shows me just how powerful the wind was—they're not that easy to pull off the hebe!

A couple of days later, we have a bright sunny autumn day. Gazing at everything glowing in the autumn light, it's a nice way to unwind after a few hours back on the ward. The sun is low above the houses over the road and peeking through the upper leaves and branches of the hebe, so I think it's south-west of here. The bit of the hebe nearest the steps to the gate is all young shoots, currently backlit and semi-translucent in the autumn glow, it's so beautiful. The crocosmia leaves are also backlit so their veins are visible and proud, still valiantly transmitting life, even as some of them are starting to brown and wither.

The red of the roses—still hanging on, the lower buds starting to bulge and get ready to open—is also catching the sun in a last-gasp show of gorgeousness. Most striking perhaps is the cotoneaster. Even though it's mostly not in the direct sunlight, the handful of yellow leaves are fiercely showing off their autumn finery. They're not ready to give in to dark winter just yet.

After a few days of gorgeous autumn sun, an all-enveloping mist descends. I can see the garden clearly, but the trees over the park, and the clock tower, are peering through the gloom of white and damp. There's definitely a nip in the air too. HD suggested buying me a heated jacket for Christmas and right now, as the damp and cold thread their way into my very bone marrow, I leap at the chance. I'll definitely appreciate a hot cup of tea when I go back indoors!

The foggy damp seeps into every crevice and joint. No matter how much I layer up, I cannot feel completely dry. Even in suburbia, the fog gives such a sense of brooding atmosphere. The sky is completely white. With no distinguishing clouds, all sense of perspective and distance is gone, there's just this flat white backdrop. All of a sudden the world is both tiny (restricted to what I can see) and infinite (whatever is beyond the white curtain).

The park trees and clock tower loom into view. It always amazes me how the same structure, the clock tower, can be so warm when it's in front of a blue sky, with sunlight flowing onto its yellow lichen cover, and yet today it is so gloomy and austere. It's not changed one bit, of course, it's my perspective that's changed, along with my mood. In the tiny garden everything is still, disarmingly so. No breeze means every branch hangs, suspended in anticipation. It's only when a sparrow comes in to check out the feeder that there's even a flicker of movement anywhere. It's like the garden is holding its breath, waiting for anything at all to happen.

The conifer is covered in droplets from the fog. This morning I thought it was frost, but nothing else was so white, so I'm pretty sure it's just water droplets reflecting the sky. It occurs to me that, although I'm interpreting this extreme stillness as anticipation, the plants will be drinking in the moisture as greedily as they can. Certainly even though it's still dull and overcast, the greens in the garden, at least the ivy and hebe and waxy-leaved bush and cotoneaster, are still as varied and vibrant as ever. I have to say, the mist and fog feel much more inspirational than the days of heavy rain when I struggle to balance brolly, pen and notebook in the gloom!

Mid-month, it's much drier, and a pale blue sky tries to break through thin white clouds, as weak rays of sunlight land on the upstairs wall of the house. The wind blows gently through the garden at just the right angle to catch one of the crocosmia plants, making it flap furiously, its leaves hitting away at itself, one of them at much greater speed than the others, like a sail flapping against its rope and mast. The movement is incongruous in a garden that is otherwise gently waving in the light breeze. The other crocosmias attempt to stand still and pretend they're not actually having to lean on a nearby surface to stay vaguely upright.

Grabbing a breather after the school run, before life admin takes over, and the sun is out, the sky is blue, but there are clouds moving in, damp in the air, and the rain isn't far away. Clearly the clouds missed the Met Office memo which, according to my app, claims a less than 5% chance of rain. I've put the umbrella up, more to protect my notebook than me. I must look so silly, as if you just looked out of the window you'd see the sky and sun but not the rain, which is too fine to perceive.

It's getting colder though, with a distinctly Scottish nip in the air. The light is dimming, with the grey clouds over the park not warmed up by their pink-white edging, and the blue of the sky definitely looking more washed out. More to the point, my fingers feel like they're about to snap off with the cold!

A burst of high pressure means that for once, even at the end of the month, we're seeing some gorgeous autumn days with blue sky and no clouds, though the chilly temperatures definitely remind me what time of year it is. If we had as many flights as usual, we'd be seeing some good 'Saltires in the sky' to herald St Andrew's Day, but mostly it's uninterrupted blue. I could honestly just sit here and look at the sky all day, that deep blue always does me the world of good.

It is freezing though! Literally, according to the car, and I've had to start scraping the windows of the car before I can drive to work. It's not yet cold enough for the lawn to be frosted, I assume it's too near the warmth of the house, as the grass lining the A9 was lovely and frost-speckled. As the month closes, the blue sky almost visible through a veil of thin white cloud casts the garden in an eerie light—brighter than grey, but definitely not sunny. Winter's on the way.

A flapping behind me reminds me I've not seen the pigeons out here for a while. I did spot a couple recently, presumably the same ones, out on the back wall having a bit of a barney. I also spotted a brief glimpse of a great tit on the peanuts earlier, so I'm happy it's still around. It's been a while since I've seen the robin and blackbirds, but as winter draws in and the feeders fill up, no doubt they'll not be far away. A sharp trilling from the rowan, an insistent 'tr-tr-tr-tr-tr-tr,' which I don't recognise. I'll have to get up slowly to not frighten it off. And I'm so glad I was careful, I turned round and think it's the robin back!

England goes back into full lockdown, and they're still counting votes in the US election. I'm refreshing the CNN website more than is probably healthy, hoping to spot movement in the Electoral College scores, but it's been Biden on 253 and Trump on 213 for ages. Can I allow myself to hope yet? Trump's going lawsuit-crazy trying to stop the vote counting, having declared himself the winner early on. Even if Biden does win, it's so close at the moment that the next few months will be a worry. I'm going to dare to hope. Many of the outstanding counts look likely to go Biden's way, judging by which states are still to declare. I don't think he'll change the world, and will no doubt be disappointing, but after the toxicity of the last four years there's still no comparison, and the relief will be palpable.

In the garden, though, life carries on regardless of world political machinations. The last two mornings at breakfast time I've spotted a magpie in the hebe. I wonder if they're the ones helping themselves to the monkey nuts, rather than the squirrels we'd assumed were taking them? Although having said that, earlier today I saw a great tit, of all tiny things, fly off with a monkey nut in its beak and come back for another. Speaking of which, right on cue a great tit arrives first for peanuts then the fatball, followed by a sparrow. They're too fast for me to be entirely confident of my tit identification, they might be blue tits, but I'll enjoy their antics whatever they are!

A huge flock of crows (I think) has just flown overhead and whirled and wheeled about directly above the garden. It's too sunny to be able to see if the photo I took was any good, but it was a good sight. Earlier today while I was in the school playground, a skein of geese flew over on their way south. I don't know why I always find that such a hopeful and inspiring sight. Nature is continuing to do what it does, despite all humanity's attempts to balls up this beautiful earth while we play our silly power games in ignorance or malice or greed.

Another day, through the mist I can hear the gulls and crows calling, Friend Cat over the road, and lots of chirping nearby from the sparrows, who have been in the garden in exuberant abundance since I filled up the feeders a couple of hours ago. I've also seen great tits and a robin, as well as one of the pigeons sitting on top of the roof over the road and seeming to stare straight into our front window at me.

Watching the birds through the window, it strikes me that the sparrows and tits have different queueing manners, it's not just their table manners that are different and distinctive. When the sparrows are at the feeder, demurely eating the seeds that are nearest, the tits seem quite happy to wait their turn, before then settling in and shovelling away at the seeds at the back and spilling whatever's in their way. The sparrows on the other hand, whilst they're comparatively tidy eaters, do not like to queue, and are pushing and shoving and flapping at each other both on the branch and even on the feeder itself! When there's a few of them there at the same time it can get quite fraught.

I can't help thinking, as I ponder tit and sparrow manners, that the stories we almost subconsciously tell about creatures (and also about other people) colour our prejudices. I tell myself without even thinking that the sparrows and tits are enthusiastic and exuberant, but the pigeons are trying to psych me out and bully everything in sight. That makes it so much harder to see all of them as just creatures trying to find food and shelter. I'm sure the stories we tell ourselves have a similar effect: about asylum seekers, long-term unemployed people and others. It stops us seeing their true humanity, wanting shelter and warmth and the best for their families like the rest of us.

While I muse on this, a jackdaw inches shiftily sideways along over-the-road's gutter, reminding me of DreamGirl's early swimming lessons where they were taught to inch along the side of the pool, and adding to my mental story-telling. I know that anthropomorphising the non-human world isn't the 'done thing,' but it's hard not to when so many of them display behaviour that can be easily mapped onto human emotion and experience. Even as I'm not entirely comfortable with ascribing human motivations and thought patterns to these wild creatures, it does also give me a feeling of connection. Affection, even.

The blackbird's back! The wing flap was so heavy I expected to see one of the pigeons, so that was a lovely surprise. It had a softer and more graceful landing on the hebe branch, so even if I couldn't see the difference in colour I would have known it wasn't a pigeon. Not to be outdone, though, a pigeon chooses this exact moment to do a scruffy flyover too! What a year it's been, when such simple things give such enormous pleasure.

The joy of the birdsong is overwhelming on an otherwise wet and soggy day. The election has finally been called for Biden, so I don't care that I'm sitting out here looking ridiculous with brolly and waterproofs. Someone on Twitter talked about it feeling like a siege had been lifted, and friends online wrote about being able to breathe easier, and I don't think these feelings should be dismissed. There's also a viral meme going about along the lines of 'live your life so the entire planet doesn't dance in the street when you lose your job.' Damn right.

The birds reflect my relief—and joy—in the cacophonous racket they're making. They're on their second pile of worms today already, and have pretty much scoffed all the seeds I put out yesterday, so they're definitely bulking up for winter. There are joyful cheeps all over the place: sparrows (I think) in our hedge and conifer, and Next Door's 'singing hedge' full of cheeping tits. I want to shout from the rooftops too!

Walking to school the next day, there is such a racket coming from somewhere near the car park that DreamGirl thinks it's a car alarm, but it's actually what sounds like hundreds of birds (sparrows, I think) in the bushes, mostly unseen, but definitely not unheard! Once we tune into the fact that we are effectively walking along a nature corridor, not just along a main road, we see nature everywhere: loads of pigeons on top of one of the blocks of flats, and seemingly every lamppost sporting a crow or seagull, peering into (or perhaps out of) the misty gloom.

A blackbird calls loudly from the rowan next door, which it is sharing with five or six sparrows. Meanwhile something has started cheeping from the hebe. A great tit, I think. Now, despite the traffic noise, I'm hearing birds from every which way. The blackbird just did a very close flypast, from the clematis just behind me over to the hebe. I felt the gust of its wings! It lets out a loud series of cheeps before flying back to the rowan, as though it's claiming its territory back. The great tit keeps its distance till the blackbird flies off, then checks out the peanuts and the seeds. I can't believe when I came out here today I thought the garden was still—I can't keep up with the birds coming and going, flying past (a sparrow just flew daringly close to me en route to the seeds), with the cheeps and peeps tinnitus-like in their intensity and constancy.

The blackbird (a juvenile, I think) is back. It must have done a circuit round the back as it appeared again from my right, flew super-close and landed on the lawn before disappearing under the sparrow hedge. The sparrows and tits are indulging in some formation flying. There's so much to see and hear, I'm grinning from ear to ear at this free display, which nine times out of ten I'm too busy to notice even though it's right on my doorstep. Oh, I love this place. I know lots of people will look at it and see 'too small, a bit scruffy, needs a good tidy,' but right now I can't imagine being anywhere else. Who needs reality TV when you can have this much entertainment at your fingertips? Excuse me while I sit and wallow in my contentment!

Three sparrows come to check out the freshly-filled feeder, and are hopping about in the conifer, which shivers at their touch. They're still full of beans despite the gloomy weather, although their calls are more subdued. Unlike them, I'm finding it hard to feel inspired. I'm happy the feeders are all filled, so the birds can get on with their winter preparations, but I feel a sense of lethargy, or even ennui, reflecting the dull conditions in the garden. It's not so much the rain, which I'm happy enough to sit out in and watch what's going on, but I'm not feeling energised today, unlike the sparrows, who've already grown in number and are having a loud squabble at the feeder. It is honestly quite hard to muster enthusiasm for much when it's this damp and grim, although a cheerful serenade from a coal tit cheers me up immediately.

The last few days I've heard a whistle, and wonder if it's the blackbird doing a descending glissando. I can definitely hear what I think is the blackbird, the song is stronger and more formed than the single peeps and cheeps of the tits and sparrows. Right on cue, a great tit lands in the hebe and Friend Cat jumps up onto the lawn to check out my legs. The sparrows have arrived in the hebe too—I think I'm probably a bit too close to the feeder for them to go there, although it didn't stop them from doing a pretty close Red Arrows-style flypast a few minutes ago.

The robin has just landed on the lawn by the feeder, another visitor that always cheers me up. This does feel like a welcoming place, despite the gloom. I find a welcome as I sit here for a few minutes to write, and I love that all these birds find it a haven too. Something (I wonder if it was the robin?) was singing a lovely song just then, over the top of the cheeps that are all around me. The robin on the lawn seems more interested in the dropped seeds than the feeder, but it's flown up quite happily into the hebe too, and the coal tits have descended again on the feeder, which will give the robin plenty more to hoover up. And now there's a loud, trilly song which I'm sure will be the blackbird, from the volume as much as the rapid melody, although it's currently out of sight.

I might be a bit glum about the dreich weather, but it's not bothering the birds by the feeder, sparrows and coal tits, and the cheeping and wing-flapping is pretty constant. The same crocosmia leaf as before is flapping like the clappers in the otherwise gentle breeze, mirroring the rush of the flapping wings as a sparrow flies low past me and others get worked up in the tree.

A bunch of starlings are starting to congregate on the top of the clock tower, around nine or ten of them. It reminds me of driving to work, the last couple of times I've driven through Plean it's looked like nearly every tree and hanging telegraph wire is covered in crows, it's quite a sight. I do like that since starting to watch more intensely what's happening in this little patch of the world, I'm starting to notice corridors of nature where I least expect them, on walls and along main roads. It gives me hope that nature is able to find places to thrive, despite us.

It's distinctly colder today, but sunny, so I'm now sitting in my current favourite spot watching the aerial acrobatics from the coal tits, sparrows and blue tits. Although I try to move my viewpoint (to the extent that I can in a few square metres!), sitting here on the paving slabs facing the bird feeder means that I get a ringside seat but am far enough away to not put them off. Right now, the sparrows are at the seed feeder and fatball, and two coal tits are chasing each other. A robin just landed in the tray to pick up the spilled seeds, and one of the pigeons lumbered overhead, looking like its chances of flying properly or falling from the sky were about fifty-fifty. I honestly can't keep up with the coal tits zooming about. They look so carefree, even as I know they're doing the very serious business of building themselves up for winter.

The acrobatic coal tit has just done a quick pole dance hanging onto the base of a crocosmia leaf. It was only a couple of seconds, but made me smile, I've not seen them do that before. It's still bouncing and flitting about, and is now joined by another one. This is honestly as entertaining as *Strictly*, they'd definitely get a ten from me!

A gull is croaking away somewhere towards the main road, but in front of me—possibly in the rowan, or over the road—are a couple of real songsmiths. Either blackbirds or robins, although I can't see them. I'm not sure if they're duelling to claim territory, or maybe they're a family group of the same bird having a bit of a singsong. I can't believe I didn't realise what beautiful singers they both were before this year.

As well as the seeds, the birds are now polishing off a fatball in around a day, so I guess they have ramped up the winter padding to see them through, as it took them two or three times that not so long ago. We've also put out a tray of leftover porridge for them and will see if they take to that.

The pigeon is on the lawn and just about manages to heave itself over the hedge and away. It really is huge. It pretty much fills the seed catcher tray now. I must admit though to feeling a little uncomfortable about focusing so much on its size (I'm hardly Skinny Minnie!), and wonder if I'm doing that in order to try and deflect my interpretation that they'd fit in more, and co-exist more freely alongside the other birds if they were less greedy and keen to push the other birds out.

A great tit briefly checked out the fatball, but other than that the birds seem pretty quiet right now. I'm hoping that saying they're quiet will have the same effect as it does on the hospital ward, where saying 'it's quiet' guarantees non-stop chaos, crises and annoyances from that point onwards. Right on cue, here come the sparrows, one at the feeder and two in the hebe. Something is singing—blackbird maybe—and now a coal tit has arrived. In the absence of enough space to grow hedges and fruiting plants to provide food for the birds, it really is a marvel the difference that putting out feeders has been, and I'm pleased that I can give them rich pickings here.

The robin has just flown into the cotoneaster undergrowth, and the pigeon has been flapping about next door (I can see it now that the sparrow hedge is starting to drop its leaves), and now I wonder if it senses me writing about it, because it has just flown right over my head, its wings barely holding it up. My hands and knees are starting to freeze out here, but I'm glad I've been able to get out here and enjoy the show.

Even at the end of November, the sparrows still have plenty of energy, and I sit down to watch the acrobatics. I am rich beyond measure to be able to see this show, that so many of us are too busy to appreciate, or even notice. The urgent song of the robin pierces the gloom. Is it calling to another, or having a moan about the acrobatic sparrows by its food? Or that woman sitting in the garden again? The sparrows fly off and the robin is straight onto the tray to pick up the fallen seeds. That always surprises me. Unlike the blackbird, the robin is hardly any bigger than the sparrows, so I thought it would comfortably manage the feeder like they do, but it much prefers picking up the fallen leftovers.

There's a shout-off going on between the sparrows in the sparrow hedge, and then whatever is in Next Door's singing hedge. They're so loud it's hard to concentrate, and both lots are going gangbusters, giving it their all. There is a brief twenty seconds where they both stop (I'm treating each collective as a single entity, I realise), but then they start again. I wonder what that's all about.

There are so many sparrows about, especially now I've refilled the feeders. Earlier through the window I saw more than I could count taking off and flying away from around the feeder, and now there's another sparrow flypast from next door. And now four sparrows from our hedge have zoomed over to next door. A good reminder that my boundaries are meaningless, their territory and vision is much bigger than just here. Another is moving about on the ground beneath the cotoneaster, and then jumps about in the inner branches of the sparrow hedge. I love that this tiny space contains such a diversity of micro-habitats. All entirely accidental, of course, I'm sure the previous owners who planted it up had no idea of the riches they were bequeathing the birds (and me).

I had to knock out ice from the water tray earlier, that's the first time since last winter that I've seen it frozen. I'll have to keep a closer eye on it, as I don't want the birds to go thirsty. I want to do as much as I can to help them get through the winter.

As the weather gets less hospitable, it feels like the plants in the garden are reflecting my mood. Of course I'm over-interpreting, but I do find it comforting to think that, like us, the plants and shrubs are tightening their belts and battening down the hatches, figuratively-speaking, by pulling the chlorophyll back inside them, and dropping leaves and flowers. The only exception seems to be the ivy, which is still merrily putting on new growth despite regular pruning. I'm probably going to have to give it another haircut soon. It's looking much like me, my pandemic hair is shaggy and scruffy too!

Next door's rowan is now pretty much bald and leafless, it's such a contrast to all the evergreens here in this garden. I'm so grateful for the scruffy but still green life here, spilling over the ramshackle borders and providing life and shelter. Even when all the roses have gone over and we say goodbye to their blousy reds, I'll be glad for the different shades and varieties of green, hinting at wild and not-quite-tamed suburbia, rather than ordered but bare beds and neat corners.

The hebe looks like it's marching forwards from the low stem that juts out at an angle near the ground, and shoots of hebe are emerging from the ivy. Earlier when I was thinking about cutting back the ivy, I realised that if I wasn't careful I'd be chopping the young hebe stalks too. Does this garden ever stop growing?! I really need to work out how to take hebe cuttings. Whenever we end up moving again, I'd so love for the same plant to be the heart of the garden again.

Next to Next Door's singing hedge, the side hedge is a lovely mix of yellow and brown leaves, with green ivy working through it, and an occasional cluster of its own light green leaves. The park trees beyond are just about bare now, but this perfect colour combination gives a sense of warmth which the weather is definitely not matching! Meanwhile the roses are still, for now, defiantly and gloriously red, still sticking two fingers up to winter. And there's even still a few tiny blobs of purple left on the lavender, its leaves light green but still luminously alive. I could do with some of that energy myself, to be honest.

The waxy-leaved shrub and the pyracantha both still have red berries too. It's bugging me that I can't remember noticing the red berries before this year. I suppose they must have been there, but what a waste of nature's bounty, even in this tiny space, that I could overlook something so cheerful.

The clematis is finally starting to shed its leaves, and the sparrow and toilet brush hedges are both showing some bald patches too. The top roses are finally starting to drop their petals, joining the rose leaves which were dropped a while ago. They're conserving their energy now, ditching any surplus drains on energy. I love though that even the stuff they ditch will rot down to provide energy for the soil and the plants to continue growing into next year. How can anyone not be inspired by the ingenuity of nature's recycling? The fungi at the base of the roses are still sitting impassively, their flat saucers sheltering next year's spores, and who knows what critters? And still the ivy throws out new shoots...

Towards the end of the month, I finally cut back the achillea. I hadn't realised until I cut it back just how much room it was taking up, it's certainly thrived this year! I can see fresh leaves at its base so I know it's healthy and will be back next year, but for the next few months the lavender and holly can get their full whack of light and rain. I've also dead-headed the top roses. There are still lower-down flowers looking good, although in this wind I doubt they'll be around much longer. Will they last till December? That would be a new record for us.

As the coal tits wheel about and chuck yet more seeds away, and the pigeon barely clears me as it flies past, I find myself drawn to looking at the ivy spreading over the ground beneath the hebe, and wonder what is going on underneath. It must be pretty dank and fusty, but I bet it's teeming with microscopic life. And probably bigger life too, but I'll try not to think too hard about that! I imagine the dark, damp, dripping walls of a troll's cave. What alliances, battles, or mutually beneficial deals will be going on as the inhabitants feast and break down the leaves and dropped bird food into rich humus? I bet it's the best, most nutrient-dense soil under there. And meanwhile here in the sophisticated human world, we're mostly blind to the life teeming on our doorstep.

I've been thinking about this little garden, and what it is I like about it so much. The other day I pulled up outside Next Door's garden, and it struck me how sterile it looked. That was the right thing for our former neighbours, they were elderly and needed something easily maintained so traditional square blocks of grass edged by beds of annuals, plus hidden bulbs, would have absolutely been the best thing. But now they're not here, the annuals have all been removed, the rowan is bare (what a godsend that has been in this pandemic), it's just flat grass and looks uninspiring. Here, I love that even with 95% green, there are so many different colours, plus things crowding and overhanging each other, so the corners aren't severe, and there's more of a sense of abundant life and growth even in this fallow season.

Scotland starts its new five tier covid response this month, and England is about to go into full lockdown for a month. I have to do a ward shift to keep my hand in, although work is being more flexible about me not coming off research completely, for which I'm very grateful. There's also been a covid case at school, although not apparently transmitted there, and DreamGirl doesn't have to isolate. It feels like everyone is bracing themselves for a long haul again, but without the adrenaline that fuelled the first lockdown. Goodness knows, everyone is so tired.

The singing hedge next door has absolutely erupted! I'm not sure if it's joyful chirping or a big old bust-up, but it's certainly loud. I'm envious of the birds—of course they are on constant survival alert (so not so different from us), but to be ignorant of covid, Trump, conspiracy theories, financial worries, emotional agonies, mental distress, well, I could do with even just a day of that. I'm probably romanticising. Of course it's hard being a little bird in this world of predators, food shortage, habitat shortage and all the rest of it. But as I watch a skein of geese fly overhead, I do envy their freedom. They know where they're going and what they need and where to find it, and don't have a hundred competing thoughts and dilemmas going round their heads. Maybe that's what I get most from being out here. A glimpse of simplicity, to give me the headspace to get on with this anything but simple life.

A grey squirrel has emerged from the conifer, walked along the top of the wall towards the hebe, then went back the way it came, presumably after clocking me sitting here. In just a few minutes I've seen so much bird and animal activity, without even turning my head. And on it goes: great tit checking out the fatballs, coal tits at the foot of the seed feeder, sparrows chirping nearby.

I think if lockdown, and sitting here regularly in the garden, has taught me anything, it's how much we miss, through being so busy and constantly trying to produce and acquire more and more stuff. So much of it is unnecessary. I have so much of what I need in this tiny spot which refills the mental and emotional well every time I sit out here. I'm getting more endorphins watching the birds dancing, breathing in the petrichor, watching the seasons changing, and just slowing down, than from constant stuff and noise. Of course I'm not unaware of my privilege, working part-time with a husband whose pay more than makes up the slack, meaning I have the luxury to do this. We've experienced a drop in income since lockdown from me having to work fewer hours than before, but we're still doing OK compared to so many—if I was worrying about getting my next meal from the foodbank, or if my job would still be there at the end of furlough, I probably wouldn't find sitting and slowing down out here either practical or soothing. But, as someone with (minor, but still not insignificant) anxiety, I can say that it's helping me manage that. Not perfectly, it's not disappeared, but I'm on a level with it and doing much better, I'm sure thanks to these regular breaks to stop and notice and, crucially, appreciate and enjoy.

It's our gorgeous girl's birthday rounding off the end of the month, and the stillness of the garden couldn't contrast more blatantly with her bouncy excitement! I'm going to try and drink in the stillness while I can, because once she's home from school there'll be precious little serenity and calm for the rest of the day. As it should be!

DECEMBER

The longest year ever is finally limping to a close, it's December AT LAST, and I noticed something very, very strange that I know for sure hasn't happened before. My ceanothus is flowering and budding again! Clearly although I think it's cold, for the plants something is going on and it's not been consistently cold enough for them to fully go into torpor, to wait out the winter. There are only two clusters of bright blue flowers open, but loads more light green buds. The end of the week is forecast to be really cold, so I think it's going to get a big shock. Hopefully the type of shock that will send it into its regular torpor, rather than the type of shock that kills off a big chunk of the plant for next year. This is worrying. Am I seeing the effects of global climate change, even in this wee patch of suburbia?

Right now the garden is still, at least on the surface. DreamGirl was reading her *Tiny* book about microbes this morning as she woke up early, and one of the factoids in there was that a teaspoon of soil contains around a billion microbes (or to put it another way, around eight teaspoons of soil will contain the same number of microbes as people in the world). Now this garden might be tiny, but there's a heck of a lot more than a teaspoon of soil even here, so I'm sitting on a universe of life right beneath my feet.

I'm feeling a bit guilty about chopping back the achillea the other week, as I saw a tweet yesterday saying that dead seed and flower heads still provide food for birds and shelter for insects. I've honestly never seen the birds go near them, and there wasn't anything obviously six-legged there, but despite leaving most of the other things alone, I still feel bad. I suppose ultimately this is all a learning experience, and next year there are probably a few things I'd do differently to enhance the natural life even more.

Everything is so still here (apart from the traffic noise, of course). The clematis looks woody and arthritic, the heather is fading, the hebe flowers are pointing their brown, dead fingers downwards, and the crocosmia leaves are getting yellower and woodier by the day. The ceanothus looks a bit stunned. The two flowers are still out, but with none of the vibrancy of blue that they shout from the rooftops in summer, and the buds, which when I first noticed them were quite a vivid yellow-green, seem faded and subdued. The ivy's still not giving up, though. There are several new yellow-green leaves on new shoots, and I have to admire its persistence!

The rose is down to just two flowers now. I'm sure this is the latest they've ever been, I think last year they'd all shed by early December. I wonder if they'll be able to hang on another week till Christmas? The crocosmia leaves are now nearly all yellow-brown, with only a couple still valiantly hanging on to the rapidly fading green. The sparrow hedge and toilet brush hedge are both nearly all twigs and sticks, with occasional leaves dotted about. The toilet brush hedge leaves are all on top like a comb-over, not covering anything or fooling anyone.

The waxy-leaved bush on the other hand is a rich, deep, thick green. When everything else is hanging on for dear life, it looks like it's just coming into its own and pulsating with life. It's also starting to spread out across the bottom of the sparrow hedge towards the compost bin, and higher up creeping closer to the seed feeder. I also noticed the other week that it's starting to grow out the other side of the wall and stick out into the pavement. Having spent the year worrying about the hebe clonking people on the head, now I need to think about pruning this one too.

The hebe is shaking its branches in the wind, and the other plants are swaying a bit, but otherwise it's quite spookily still and dark, like the whole garden is hunkering down to sit out the rain. Often when it rains there are patterns of raindrops on the blades of grass, but today everything is just sodden and drenched, and I'm going to have to find beauty elsewhere. The remaining roses are starting to shed their petals, and the sparrow hedge and clematis have just a handful of yellow leaves gamely, but ultimately futilely, hanging on in there. They look how I feel.

The first appearance of the robin this month, and this time rather than sing it's muttering a gentle 'pip-pip-pip' as it hops about at the base of the feeder. Hello, little thing—I love seeing you about, it always does my heart good even though the books all tell me you're a bit of a grumpy garden thug! It's now pip-pip-pipping in the smelly bush, and a coal tit has just checked out a few seeds on the ground from the feeder, so it looks like Stirling's best-fed birds won't be far away and will be coming in for their regular gorging soon! The robin has started on the seed tray, a sparrow has zoomed low overhead to the hedge. At least as far as the birds are concerned, it's situation normal. That ceanothus flowering has got me worried though. What other of our pollen-rich plants round here are risking an ice-scorching, and how will that affect our bees and butterflies next year?

One of the pigeons attempted a flyover from the hedge, but changed its mind and did a quick U-turn. Meanwhile some sparrows are in the conifer and checking out the very squelchy lawn. They're like formation dancers, or acrobats, ascending and descending and hopping around—it really is beautiful.

The birds are appreciating the feeder now that it's cold and grim. I've seen at least six sparrows, possibly more, but they were flitting about too quickly to count them accurately, and I can hear even more. There were some tits in the melee as well, and I think that all the birds are getting more desperate now. The sparrows look noticeably bigger than before, so hopefully they'll have a successful winter.

Even though they're desperate for seeds though, I do still have to regularly wash the feeders. The last thing I want is them picking up diseases from a mucky feeder. They look to have packed on enough that a day with a bit less food won't hurt.

There's a bit of hopping about in the conifer, the sparrows have just done a spectacular low flypast (I could feel the breeze overhead in their wake), and the robin is hopping about all around the lawn, which has cheered me up no end. It's having a right good look round the base of the cotoneaster, and seems to have found something to eat. I wonder if it's the worms that are so attracted to the compost bin, as it's spending a lot of time around there.

The coal tit arrived on the smelly bush, saw no feeder so scooted up to the hebe then back for a mealworm or three. Meanwhile I caught a glimpse of the blackbird in the hebe too. Has my sitting out here created some sort of Pavlovian reaction? They see me and assume there's a full feeder of seeds.

The robin is coming close now, probably only about two feet away from my feet before flying up to the peanut tray. And now a gaggle of sparrows have landed in the hebe. So much for me thinking a few minutes ago that a missing feeder would mean fewer birds. The robin's now having a go at the fatball, and—hello blackbird!—the beautiful blackbird, a male with his gorgeous bright yellow beak, almost the only brightness right now, is hopping round the base of the feeder. The robin is all of a sudden checking out the base of the honeysuckle, I didn't even see it fly across the garden in front of me, and now it's on the steps only a foot away from where I'm sitting! I can barely move or breathe, but then someone walks past the gate and spooks it, and it flies to the relative safety of the cotoneaster.

So much activity in just fifteen minutes! Routine for the birds, just like my routine of washing and washing up and making beds and all that makes sure I'm nice and cosy with my family. But this routine goes on all day for them, and we miss so much. I'm grateful this year that I've had the chance to learn again how it doesn't take much at all to have an area teeming with life.

Back out here again, and a coal tit is flitting about and the robin is waiting under the sparrow hedge. The sun has emerged from behind a small cloud, and suddenly the blue of the sky is more concentrated, and the garden is suffused with warm light which emphasises the depths of the different greens. Now a couple of sparrows and a great tit have shown their faces, briefly, and the robin 'hides' (in much the same way that DreamGirl used to hide when we played hide and seek when she was younger, absolutely in plain sight!) on the lower stem of the smelly bush. It feels like they're all coming to say hello, even though, realistically, they're more likely coming to say 'fill these feeders already!' After a dull morning at work it's so good to see them.

The robin and one of the sparrows seem to be posturing a bit at each other, not keen at all to share the ground underneath the feeder, even though it's sodden and there's surely minimal pickings for either of them. A good reminder to me that, even as I find tranquility and refuge here, it's not all sweetness and light.

There's movement behind the twigs of the sparrow hedge, three sparrows are hopping about, doing who knows what? All three of them then zoom out over my head towards next door. I love those little bursts of frenetic energy, even as I feel I'm wading through treacle at the end of the year, just trying to get through to the holidays and Christmas so we can all recharge and rest.

And the conifer is singing! I can't see any birds, but there are definitely at least two in there singing and cheeping their hearts out, it does me such good to hear it. There's a blue tit hopping about the upper branches of the hebe. It's been on the fatball quite a lot today already. There's also something—a coal tit, I think, although it's a bit far away to make out for certain—in Next Door's rowan, and I can hear gulls behind me too. There's also a fat pigeon on top of a chimney pot on the corner, goodness knows how it managed to get up there! I am definitely feeling watched!

The coal tits have now arrived at the fatball and seeds for their turn. I think I caught a glimpse of the robin too behind the seed feeder, though it was only fleeting and could have been a sparrow. I can hear what sounds like seeds being cracked by a beak, but couldn't see any birds until I caught the tiniest movement, high up in the hebe, of a tit (coal tit, I think), pecking away at the branch. Now the blue tits and sparrows have arrived, and yes, there's the robin peeking out on the lawn. So now I just need the blackbird and I'll have seen all our regulars in the space of just a few minutes. The blackbird is being a bit more bashful at this end of the year, but I expect it's not too far away. Meanwhile, the coal tits are peeping and the blue tits are chittering away to each other. I wish I knew what they were communicating.

A couple of great tits are having a minor stooshie in the hebe before flying off. Nothing serious, it seems. Talking of stooshies, I wonder if I'll see the robin today? There's still red in the garden from the valiant last two roses and a palmful of pyracantha berries, but that orange breast is always a welcome flash of colour.

As well as the birds dancing about in the branches, a fat pigeon flies over the sparrow hedge and then does a U-turn and heads straight back to Next Door's garden. The sparrows do a single file flypast above me back to the conifer. I envy them their energy; I am starting to seize up with the cold, so I'll leave them to it! I wish I could bottle their energy.

Boxing Day winds mean the tit on the peanut feeder has to hang on like a cowboy on a bucking bronco. The next day though, and what a difference—talk about calm after the storm! Blue sky, barely a cloud, plants mostly still apart from the tiniest movement. I've already seen the blackbird, and a great tit has just arrived to check out the new fatball and from there to the peanuts. It doesn't matter that I've been watching the same set of birds all year, it never gets boring and makes me so happy to see the feeders being so well used.

The great tit is now trilling away from Next Door's rowan, right on top of the highest branch. I assume the trilling means 'new fatballs, guys!' rather than an aria to the winter sun, but either way it's balm to my soul.

I can hear crows too, I think from the direction of the clock tower, and cheeping from the singing hedge in the other direction. I'm trying (not completely successfully) to zone out the traffic hum, but there's no way I can zone out the pigeon that lumbered overhead, first into the middle of the road, and now just watching me from the top of the gate. The wind ruffles through its feathers, but it doesn't seem bothered. I'm starting to notice the wind getting close to my skin, and it's bothering me a lot more!

The conifer's casting a solid shadow on the white wall above the toilet brush hedge, making the garden look a lot warmer than it feels. And now a coal tit is flitting about, while the pigeon (which had retreated next door when I tried to take its photo) reappears over the hedge, takes one look at me and does another U-turn. A couple of sparrows are on the smelly bush, the pigeon tries again but as I'm still here it U-turns again. Now it's landed on one of the lower hebe thick branches, just above the wall. I don't know if it thinks I can't see it. And a third U-turn over the hedge. I hope I have the same repellent effect on covid once I have my jag!

The sparrows and a coal tit are going nuts in the conifer. What a racket they're making. They'll skitter when they see the pigeon, which is back on the hebe, but I think they're growing a bit bolder and not letting it bully them so much. A solitary sparrow, almost camouflaged in amongst the mud and brown hebe leaves, is dotting about the lawn near the feeder. I'm so happy this little spot is providing them such rich pickings.

We had the tiniest dusting of snow overnight. It's already fast disappearing from the lawn and by the house, although it's still crunchy underfoot on the road and pavement. The robin fossicks about on the grass, joined by a sparrow in the conifer and a pigeon flying overhead. What's left of the snow on the grass reminds me of that delicate 'wedding ring' Shetland lace—very apt for today as it's our wedding anniversary. After thirteen years, the memory of that day still makes me so very happy. I'm celebrating it by getting my first covid jag. Who says I don't know how to do romance? I wish HD could have his too, but because of my work in the NHS I am considered a priority, whereas he will just have to get his in due course because of his age! Being a bit older than him, I am enjoying the rare chance to make an age-related joke at his expense!

The conifer still has a light icing sugar dust of snow. The roof of the church hall is whiter and wouldn't be out of place on a Christmas card, and whilst the clock tower doesn't seem to have much snow, the lichen on the cupola below the weather vane has a crisp, frozen look to it. The blackbird watches me from the rowan branches, a sparrow pokes about at the base of the feeder. Further away, cheeps carry on the thin still air as the robin surprises me from behind and saunters past my chair.

For the first time I've seen a bird (in this case the robin) rootling about in the ground ivy, picking up what looked like a bit of suet fallen from the fatball. And now the sparrow and robin are joined by the blackbird, while the pigeon flies ineffectually around the hebe and then watches me from the top of the gate. I manage to get a not great phone snap of the robin and blackbird which I'm pleased about. It won't win any awards, but will help cement the memory. The robin's now right at my feet, under the chair, and now on the doorstep, then on the rose, right by my shoulder, but nowhere long enough for me to take a picture. I'll just have to cement that memory in writing.

Lots of the birds are flying over. A sparrow and the blackbird are in the rowan, and sparrows and (I think) great tits are zooming around overhead. The robin ignores them all as it concentrates on the ground and the lower hebe branches. A slight movement over the feeder, and the flash of a yellow beak. The blackbird is at the water and worms. The robin jumps down suddenly from the hebe to the ground, making me jump—even though I know it's there, it still has the capacity for surprise. A sparrow shouting match is in full flow from the rowan. These birds are in fine form. What a brilliant start to the day this has been.

This afternoon I'll make a new batch of fatballs as the last one has just been polished off. The robin's already hopping about to say hello, there's a magpie on the roof of the church hall, and I can hear a high-pitched 'peep' somewhere behind me. Life is going on. Ooh hello, here's a sparrow and a coal tit at the feeder, and the blackbird hopping and poking about on the ground underneath the waxy-leaved bush—nearly all our regulars to help me see out the year.

The rain patters gently on the brolly, but doesn't feel intrusive. There's some traffic noise. Not too loud, thankfully—and suddenly a cacophonous cheeping from the sparrows in the conifer. The hebe is still, it's the waxy-leaved bush and smelly bush in particular shuddering from all the birds jumping about their branches. The chorus is getting louder and louder. Maybe they're trying to shoo off the robin, which doesn't seem remotely bothered by them, although it has retreated to the cotoneaster for a bit. They neither know nor care that it's the last day of the year. For them, it's another day to survive and thrive.

The whole country is pretty subdued. In England, the government announced London and much of the south-east are going into tier four lockdown, and the much-vaunted five days relaxation of the covid rules over Christmas will now just be one day. Meanwhile, here in Scotland we'll be going into lockdown on Boxing Day for three weeks, we'll have a week and a half[1] of home schooling, and who knows what else to come? For us, it's not really affecting our Christmas, we're so far away from family that we have an alone Christmas most years anyway, but having not seen family for a year and a half, this is feeling emotionally harder than usual. Hopefully a few tits and sparrows will cheer me up—unlike the rain which has just started falling from the BLUE SKY! What's all that about?!

---

1. Footnote from the future: this ended up being a month and a half of lockdown, and felt every bit as hard as the first one, maybe because we knew this time how miserable we'd be and we didn't have the benefit of spring weather this time.

With news of the first covid vaccine being approved at the start of the month, it feels like although it's not the end, it might be the beginning of the end, and I can't help but feel a pinprick of hope as we wait. How very Advent! I also managed to get a bit of extra work which makes me happy about being able to contribute more to the household, and so I choose to feel positive, despite the general dreichness of the weather.

The postie caught me sitting out in the murk, and asked if it wasn't too cold to be sitting out.

I just replied how much I loved it out here to help clear my head.

He seemed to get it rather than thinking I was mad: 'Aye, a bit o' tranquillity.'

Yes, that's exactly it.

My head does feel like it needs a little clearing, with a close family member in hospital in England after a fall. It's hard to know, being so far away, how much we should be worrying. Although I love living up here and have no desire to move back to England, it's times like these when I most feel the distance from our loved ones, and our impotence and inability to do anything practical to help feels most acute.

I feel too tired and fed up to stay out here. Covid fatigue (as in being tired of the whole covid thing, not tired from covid) is starting to creep in, I've had enough of it all and just want it to be over. I'm looking forward to 2021, despite it starting with a lockdown. But today, I just can't muster any enthusiasm, although the robin landing on the smelly bush at exactly this moment has at least cheered me up and I choose to interpret it as a small sign of hope. Thanks, little thing!

Apart from the birds dancing about in the branches, the garden is stock still. Like me, it's slowed right down. It feels more 'watchful' than me though. I'm reminded of a conductor frozen in his upbeat, we'll be waiting a while before the downbeat signifies the start of movement again.

And now for my last entry in this diary... We've made it to 2021, after the year like no other, and I expect things will stay bad for a while before getting better. I think the second covid vaccination dose is going to be delayed as they try to give everyone partial coverage sooner. Rates of covid infections are still high, with a new highly-infectious variant, and whilst most people are being sensible, enough aren't to make the hospitals struggle to keep up. We've a week more of school holidays and then a week of home learning but I wouldn't be at all surprised if that is extended and we go into a stricter lockdown again. I'm feeling a bit anxious about how to juggle the things I need to while HD is working and DreamGirl is at home, with no informal childcare available to us, but I'm also choosing to face the year with hope.

Life goes on, in the world as in the garden, and if this garden year has taught me nothing else, it's taught me that I have enough. I don't need to strive for more stuff or more recognition. I can strive to make what I have the best I can, to make what I am the best I can be, to fulfil the creative call, and to be content with my lot. If, as part of that, I can make the world better for others, so much the better.

The light is starting to lower, so as I close the page on this year, a few thoughts about what I've learnt out here in the garden.

I'm not as Earth Mothery as I thought, and my feelings about the pigeons in particular actually shock and trouble me a lot! Calling them fat hasn't made me a better person either. I don't think I'll ever love them instinctively, but I hope that this year has opened me to appreciating the value of every living thing, even the less obviously cute ones.

I have felt both part of the garden—shaping it through things I've planted and cut back, and through feeding and encouraging the birds—but also an outsider. Not fully understanding entirely what I'm seeing, not being able to name every bird or plant, makes me feel a step removed from it all. I want to belong, to be part of this little natural community, and to the community of writers who bring nature alive for others. But I also appreciate being able to make the unknown a bit more accessible and relatable; maybe one of the keys is not knowing it all.

One of the things I expected at the start of the year was that being in nature would make me feel good, more attuned to the world, a better person with hopefully improved mental health. And that has happened, in spades, but it's also unsettled me and made me realise how much further I need to go: in knowledge, in attitude, in care. But ultimately, this year has started to show me what's possible—the importance of caring for and appreciating the little bits of nature around me, as a first response to the potentially catastrophic future for the big nature around the world. And for that, I will be forever grateful for this tiny garden, which has taught and nurtured me beyond my wildest dreams.

ACKNOWLEDGEMENTS

There are, as is always the case with these things, an awful lot of people I need to thank for their part in getting this book to the point of publication. Although there is only my name on the cover, writing a book is never an entirely solo endeavour.

Massive thanks must go to the wonderful Julian Barr, who edited the book with care and precision. In the (admittedly rather niche) Venn diagram of academics who are also brilliant at creative writing, excellent editors, and nicest guys on the internet, he is definitely slap bang in the middle of the diagram. I so appreciated his thoughtful and interested engagement with my work, as well as his sterling suggestions for the book blurb. Of course, it goes without saying that any remaining howlers are all my own work and responsibility.

To the writing community that has sprung up round The Bestseller Experiment podcast, where can I even start? Your enthusiasm, ideas, humour, encouragement, and inspiration truly worked wonders keeping me on track with writing when giving up would have been so much easier. To the two Marks, Mr Stay and Mr Desvaux, who created this amazing community, thank you from the bottom of my heart; I have made so many good friends thanks to your mad idea to write and publish a book. And to the members of the BXP team, you're brilliant, and watching you go from strength to strength as you write and publish has been a joy.

To the amazing team at GetCovers, thank you for producing such a beautiful book cover, I'm delighted and in awe of your creativity and ability to run with my vague ideas and produce something so much better than I could ever have imagined.

To Kathryn Aalto, writing teacher extraordinaire, and my fellow students on her Art of the Personal Essay and Nature Writing courses, thank you for such constructive and inspirational teaching and feedback. You gave me the confidence and belief that I had a story to tell, and the tools to help me tell it. I'm proud to be one of your alumni.

To my family, friends, and colleagues, who periodically asked how the book was going, thank you for believing in me and this project even when you had minimal evidence that it was anything other than a vague dream. Your continued interest encouraged me to keep plugging away, and I'm so happy I can now say the book is a reality!

Most especially, my thanks and love to HD and DreamGirl. It was a rough old year in 2020, and I'm sure there were times when I was sitting out in the garden in the rain when you must have thought I'd finally lost it. But I wouldn't have got through the year, or this book, without you both. I love you, you're the best.

About the Author

Jackie Kirkham has lived in Scotland since 2005, and can't imagine living anywhere else. She is a research nurse and former academic, and proud nerd. The Calm Place is her first book.

AUTHOR NOTE

If you enjoyed this book, I'd be so grateful for a review on your online retailer of choice. Reviews are one of the best ways you can show your appreciation for an author's work, and a good review will always make our day! Thank you!

If you would like to keep up to date with my writing and news, as well as recommendations for other books, art and resources relating to the natural world, you are very welcome to sign up to my author newsletter. As a thank you from me, everyone who signs up will receive a free 'Nature Noticing' worksheet, which could be used for inspiration for your own writing, or simply a prompt to stop and find new ways to appreciate the nature on your own doorstep. The newsletter sign-up form is available from https://subscribepage.io/sAO2Yk. You can also contact me via my website, jackiekirkham.co.uk/

I look forward to connecting with you!

Correction

Please note that the link to subscribe to my newsletter has now changed to
https://jackiekirkham.substack.com

Hope to see you there!

Milton Keynes UK
Ingram Content Group UK Ltd.
UKHW012059240823
427342UK00003B/58